FLIGHT FROM LEDRON

T0351675

Diana Noonan

Published by Pearson Education Limited, Edinburgh Gate, Harlow, Essex, CM20 2JE
Registered company number: 872828

www.pearsonschools.co.uk

First published by Pearson
a division of Pearson New Zealand Ltd
67 Apollo Drive, Rosedale, North Shore 0632, New Zealand
Associated companies throughout the world

Text © Pearson 2007

Designed by Sarah Healey

The right of Diana Noonan to be identified as author of this work has been asserted
by her in accordance with the Copyright, Designs and Patents Act 1988.

First published 2007
This edition published 2012

21
10 9

British Library Cataloguing in Publication Data
A catalogue record for this book is available from the British Library

ISBN 978-0-43507-613-9

Acknowledgements
We would like to thank the children and teachers of Bangor Central Integrated
Primary School, NI; Bishop Henderson C of E Primary School, Somerset; Brookside
Community Primary School, Somerset; Cheddington Combined School,
Buckinghamshire; Cofton Primary School, Birmingham; Dair House Independent
School, Buckinghamshire; Deal Parochial School, Kent; Lawthorn Primary School,
North Ayrshire; Newbold Riverside Primary School, Rugby and Windmill Primary
School, Oxford for their invaluable help in the development and trialling of the Bug
Club resources.

Every effort has been made to contact copyright holders of material reproduced in
this book. Any omissions will be rectified in subsequent printings if notice is given
to the publishers.

A division of Pearson New Zealand Ltd

Contents

Chapter One

"You've found something. Tell me what it is or I'll report you."

Amon's head jerked up. The girl from Division Three was staring down at him.

"Nothing," he lied. "I haven't found anything."

"I saw you," she hissed. "I was watching when you went off for a pee. On the way back you stopped by a rock. You picked something up."

"Nah, I was just doing up my boot."

"You shoved it under your jacket," she continued. "Tell me what it is or I'll call the Secure Division over."

Amon felt a tightness in his stomach and knew it was fear. If anything unusual was discovered while the Divisions were out on a well-dig, it had to be reported immediately. If anything was withheld, there would be consequences.

His tongue circled his lips nervously. How much time did he have before she signalled one of the guards? If he told her the truth, would she keep it to herself? He had no reason to think so, except that she wasn't any ordinary girl.

"How come you're the only female in your Division?" he stalled.

"I'm tough," she replied. "I topped my physical tests."

"So you're on maximum water rations?"

"You bet — and I work for every drop. Now, are you going to show me what you found?"

Inside his overalls the injured creature moved. It was a bird, he was almost sure of it. Its covering was sleek and smooth except for a sticky patch where blood had seeped from the wound in its leg. Its tiny jewelled eyes had stared at him in fear as he lifted it up and, as he held it briefly in his hands, he had felt the frantic beating of its heart.

Amon had never seen a bird — not a real one. He had never seen an animal at all, except on-screen in the library archives. Animals were enemies — not that they were thought to exist any more. In a world without adequate water supplies, they had been viewed by the first Leaders as a danger, competition for resources so limited that human life was barely sustainable. It was said in the history files that, in the first few years after the community of Ledron was established, a lone animal roaming the desert would sometimes venture within the outer boundaries of the compound, an escapee from some misguided settlement that still saw usefulness in this form of life. The Secure Division dealt with them hastily.

Animals were considered enemies, so why had Amon not reported the find? He searched inside himself for an answer and couldn't find it. Except that the bird was something so strange, almost magical, that he wanted, for a little while, to keep it, to observe it. It fascinated him that something non-human could move and breathe, that it could be so different to himself and yet be a living thing. He had to keep it — for a little while, anyway.

"I'll show you what I've found later," he told her. "If you shut up about it, I'll show you when we're back at the settlement."

"But you're not allowed to . . ."

"It's amazing," he said. "You've never seen anything like it. It's alive, it moves, it's warm, but it's not like us."

"You've found an *animal*!" The girl's eyes were wide with astonishment. "You've found an . . ."

"Don't you want to see it?" he asked. "Aren't you curious? It might be the only time in your life that you ever see one. Don't you want to touch it?"

She stared at him. Tiny beads of perspiration were gathering along the top of her lip. Her eyes darted this way and that as if she was trying to make a decision.

"It's so unreal," he said. "It's got legs and a sort of face and this white covering of something — not like skin, more like . . . like fabric."

For a moment he saw real curiosity in her face.

"Show it to me now!" she demanded.

"Later," said Amon. "I'll show you later."

"No!" she said suddenly. "I'm not in on this with you. Do you hear me? I don't want anything to do with it."

"But you won't call the guards?"

"I don't want to know anything about what you've found. Forget I ever spoke to you — do you understand?"

"You mean . . ."

"I *never* spoke to you."

"Okay, okay," said Amon. "I understand."

She turned on her heel and began walking away.

"What's your name?" Amon called after her. "Where are you located?"

"Hester," she replied, without turning back. "Don't try to contact me."

Amon looked at his watch. It was only two in the afternoon. There were three more hours of digging to do before the march home and it would be impossible to work with the creature stowed under his overalls. Then he had an idea. He would tuck the creature into his jacket, which he'd left lying on the ground. He would zip it into the inner pocket and hope it didn't make a noise or move about so much that it drew attention to itself. As an added precaution, he would leave the jacket tucked in the lee of a rock.

"You got a problem?" asked one of the Secure Division when Amon returned from stowing the bird. "Lost something?"

"No," said Amon hastily. "I was just getting my skin cream from my jacket. I think I'm getting some sort of rash."

"You want to go back — get it checked out?"

"Nah, I'll be fine. I'll call at the Med Centre tonight. It's probably nothing."

There was no way Amon could risk going back to the settlement early. If he did, he would be accompanied by one of the Secure Division guards. If the animal made some sort of noise, it would immediately be noticed. It would be safer if he went home that night in the regular group. The noise of talking and joking would drown out any unusual sound.

Chapter Two

That afternoon, Amon was on winch duty. The new well was only twenty metres deep but they were already hauling out thirty buckets of spoil every fifteen minutes. It took Amon and two others to wind the winch. The rest of the workers were down the hole with picks and shovels. With any luck, they'd sink the new well in three months.

"I like the look of that wind," said Marco, as he and Amon tugged on the handle of the winch. "It's as strong as it gets and it's coming straight from the south, regular as can be — none of that pathetic gusting we had last week."

"Are you taking out a yacht tonight?" asked Amon.

Marco grinned. "You bet. I've got a time trial in two weeks and I'm aiming to cut the record by three seconds."

Amon nodded. "Good luck. If anyone can do it, you can."

Marco was sixteen, a couple of years older than Amon, and the best sand-yachter in his age group. He'd clocked up fifty kilometres an hour on the dry, flat plain that stretched out for a hundred kilometres around the compound — not that anyone was allowed to go out that far. The yacht track was an oval circuit five kilometres long. You could go as fast as you liked — or could — as long as you didn't leave the circuit.

"Want to come with me?" asked Marco.

Amon answered as casually as he could. "Nah, I'm busy."

"Meeting someone interesting?" asked Marco. "I saw you talking with that girl. Hester, isn't it?"

"Yeah, I think that's her name. And, no, I'm not seeing her. I'm going to the gym. Got to keep fit if I'm staying in this Division."

"I know what you mean," said Marco. "That extra water ration at night is worth having."

Marco was right. In a world where every milli-litre of water was rationed, the extra half-litre of water that Well Division workers were allocated was worth working for. It was only given to well-diggers who worked to a grade five standard. And, apart from Hester, they were all male.

Amon looked up at the cloudless sky. It was the colour of ash and, beneath it, in every direction, dry, cracked earth stretched out in one gigantic plain. How there could be even a drop of water under it was a mystery.

On the way home that evening, the Secure Division guard Amon had spoken to came over to talk to him.

"How's that rash?" he asked.

"Not so bad," Amon replied.

"I've made a note that you'll call at the Medical Centre this evening."

"Sure," Amon said. "Thanks. I won't forget."

Amon wasn't sure why he didn't like the guards from the Secure Division. They were there, after all, to look after the welfare of everyone in the community. That's why they came out on the well-digs: to check that the job went smoothly, that there were no dangerous practices developing, that everyone received the correct ration of water at break times. But Amon sensed another side to them, one that was kept just under the surface, so that you couldn't really identify it.

Amon remembered the time that Luther, a guy he knew vaguely from seeing him in the library, had one day wandered away from a well-dig and headed out across the desert. A Secure Division guard had gone after him. Amon had watched them from a distance. At first there had been some sort of discussion. Then the guard had become rough, propelling Luther back — not to the group of well-diggers, but to the compound. Amon hadn't seen Luther after that and, when he'd asked one of the guards about him, he'd been told that Luther was working in another Division on the east side of Ledron. But Amon hadn't seen Luther at the library again, not once. After the "incident", he hadn't seen him at all.

A mean wind was gathering real force as the Divisions approached the settlement. Sand and grit whipped at Amon's legs and he squinted to keep the dust from his eyes. Marco was still talking about the wind.

"Come on, Amon, why don't you come sailing? I could teach you, you know."

Against Amon's chest, the bird was soft and warm. So, you're still alive, he thought. He turned to Marco. "I've told you before, it scares me."

"Just because you saw a sailor get his leg caught in the mainsheet when you were little. That was years ago. You have to get over it."

"He got dragged for metres. No, there's no way I want to sail."

"Too bad," said Marco. "It's so good once you're out there in the wind."

The bird moved and Amon wished desperately that he could reach into his pocket and feel its silky covering. He tried hard to think of the word for it, and then remembered. It was "feathers". That's what he'd read in the library. Animals had had different coverings. Some had fur, which was a thick, soft fibre; others had hair, which was a little like the hair on his mother's head; and then there were birds. They had the strangest covering of all: sharp stalks that poked from their skin and, on each side of every stalk, fans of soft, shiny material. The whole structure was called a feather and there were hundreds on each animal. But more amazing than anything else was the fact that these strange creatures possessed the ability to fly through the air.

Amon looked up at the sky. When he was little he'd flown kites and watched them dance in the breeze. They'd tugged and tugged and wanted to escape but they were harnessed to a line and could never choose where they flew. But birds, they could fly wherever they wanted to go. They were free.

Amon looked about at the lines of tired well-diggers marching home. What would it be like to be free — to fly away from all of this?

Chapter Three

Amon's mother was sweeping their courtyard when he got home. Her long, brightly coloured earrings swung back and forth as she pushed the broom over the mosaic of flat stones.

"Hello, my strong boy," she said. She smiled and rested her chin on the handle of the broom.

Amon smiled back. "I'm tired," he said, quickly heading for his room before she gave him a hug. "I want to get cleaned up and have a rest before we eat."

Lydia raked the fingers of one hand through her short, spiky grey hair. For a moment, Amon saw a look of worry in her eyes.

"There was something I wanted to talk to you about," she began.

"Can't it wait?" Amon knew that he'd snapped but he had to make it clear to her that he really wanted to be by himself for a while.

She tried to smile again, but this time her lip trembled. Then she nodded firmly. "Right," she said. "We'll talk later."

Amon went into his room, closed the door and slid the bolt across the latch. Gently, he lifted the jacket over his head and laid it on his bed. Then he zipped open the pocket and reached inside for the bird.

"It's all right," he whispered, and then realised with a start that he was actually talking to the animal. The blood from its wound was smeared across its chest.

He laid the bird on the bed. It was as long as his foot and its feathers were pure white where they weren't stained with blood. As Amon looked at it, its dark eyes blinked and its beak opened wide.

It's thirsty, he thought. How long was it since it had drunk? For the first time since he had found it, it occurred to Amon that he would have to give the bird water. But how was he supposed to do that? Water was the most carefully guarded commodity in Ledron. Water had to be collected and drunk in front of a member of the Secure Division. That way no one could stockpile it in their home or share their own ration with another member of the family.

Amon knew the rules and the reasons for them. There was just enough water for each person to survive. But, if family members were showing signs of illness, and weren't able to collect their own rations, their loved ones might be tempted to take water to them instead of reporting their condition to the Care Division.

Amon shuddered. It was the job of the Care Division to make decisions about anyone who became ill. If an ailment was minor and the patient required little nursing before they were able to return to work, assistance would be given. If the illness was serious or terminal, it was, in the words of the Leaders, necessary for the good of all that the patient be "retired". Amon's father had been "retired" when Amon was still a baby.

The bird opened its beak again. It was gasping. There was no time to lose. Amon wrapped the animal loosely in his jacket and placed it under his bed, against the far wall.

"Amon?" said Lydia, when he came out into the courtyard.

"I'm going to get water," he said quickly.

"But I thought we could talk now."

"I'm really thirsty," he said abruptly, seeing the hurt in her eyes. Amon didn't like treating her like this and he knew she would think his behaviour strange. They were close, he and Lydia. Many people didn't care much about their families, but Amon and his mum were good friends. Perhaps it was because there was just the two of them that they shared everything: feelings, news, hopes . . . But he couldn't tell her about the bird, not yet. First he had to decide what he thought about it himself.

In the water room, Amon tapped his personal code into the dispenser. "It is Tuesday April 31 2107," came the automated response through the speaker. "You have two point five litres of water available."

"I'll have two hundred and fifty mils," said Amon clearly, into the receiver.

He held his cup under the dispenser and watched the water trickle into it. He walked along to the Secure Division guard sitting behind the counter and raised the cup to his lips. He saw the guard studying his throat to see that he was swallowing.

The guard nodded and Amon nodded back. Then he walked swiftly from the room. It wasn't difficult to hold the few millilitres of unswallowed water in his mouth, as long as no one wanted him to speak. He rushed back to his room with his head down. Fortunately, Lydia wasn't waiting for him.

Inside his room, Amon spat the saved water back into his cup. Then he reached under the bed for the bird. Holding it in his lap, he tipped the water toward its beak. The bird suddenly became more alive. It slipped its beak into the cup, scooped up the water, then lifted its head back and up to swallow. It did it again and again, until the cup was empty.

Amon wanted to offer it more, but it was too soon to go back to the water room. Requesting another ration so soon after the last was sure to arouse suspicion. The creature would have to wait.

Amon sat on the bed, studying it. It was so light, so fragile. Although it seemed very tired and kept closing its eyes, its lids would suddenly blink open at the slightest sound. Amon tried to imagine himself in a strange situation, in a place he hadn't been before, injured and with someone he hadn't yet learned to trust.

"Maybe you'd like to be by yourself, in the dark," he whispered to the bird. "But first I have to look at your wound."

Gently, he hoisted the bird on to his lap and carefully studied its injured leg. A short, jagged tear was visible in the skin. Amon wondered what had made it.

In the past, long before he was born, the guards of the Secure Division had used guns to shoot wandering animals. But there *were* no animals now, and no other communities out there in the desert — that's what the Leaders told them. They were so sure of it that they no longer sent guards to patrol the outer perimeters of the settlement. Now there was nothing and no one in the whole world except for Ledron itself. And it existed only because of the wisdom of the Leaders, whose knowledge of water conservation had enabled life to continue as it did.

Amon looked down at the bird. But, if all that was true, where had the bird come from? Perhaps the Leaders were misinformed? But that was impossible; they were all-knowing. Unless they were hiding some knowledge that only they possessed? Amon tried to dismiss the thought from his mind.

He took a soft cleansing cloth from its container beside his bed. He was allocated three a day for personal hygiene. Females, who were not required to shave off all their hair, received an extra ration for a hair-cleansing once a week.

With a corner of the cloth he wiped the dried blood, cemented with sand, from the bird's leg. It struggled a little, and he worked more carefully. The wound was soon looking clean but raw. With the rest of the cloth, he delicately wiped the bird's feathers. As he worked, the creature seemed to relax, to accept that he meant it no harm.

"Now I'm going to put you back under the bed," he murmured. He took a storage cube from his cupboard and lined it with one of his shirts. Then he placed the bird inside, covered the cube with another shirt, and pushed the container under the bed again.

For a moment, he relaxed. The bird was safe, it had drunk. Time was on his side. He would go to the library before the evening meal and try to find out as much as he could about the animal, especially about what it ate.

Chapter Four

Outside, it was quiet. Pre-mealtime was when everyone relaxed after their work, when families gathered in their stone houses to share the stories of their day or to listen to the Leaders' news briefs on their house screens.

Amon hurried along the cobbled alleyway. High above him, the giant windmills whirred gently, generating Ledron's power. At the door of the library, he peered inside. There was no one around. He clicked open the door and went in. The infoputers hummed in the semi-darkness.

"Password" flashed across the screen of the machine he had chosen. Amon tapped in his code. For the first time, he felt uncomfortable — as if his actions might be being monitored. He told himself that it was ridiculous, that there was no reason why anyone would want to know what he was up to or what he was interested in. Ledron wasn't a prison, he wasn't an inmate, a slave. He was, like everyone else, working for his own survival, so that life could be as good as it was possible to be in the desert that the world had become.

Amon typed "bird" into the search panel, and a general description of that animal family appeared. He would have to narrow the search to identify the bird he had found. He worked quickly and steadily, rapidly scanning screen after screen of information. He was so absorbed in his work that it wasn't until he heard the click of the library door closing that he realised he was no longer alone in the room. He spun round.

"Hester!"

"What are you doing here?" she asked. "But you don't need to tell me. I can guess."

"I know what it is. I've identified what I found."

"I told you, I don't want to know."

"Then why are you here?"

"I came to look for some information for a maths assignment I'm working on. I'm going for my G-levels before the end of the month."

He swallowed hard. So, she wasn't just strong, she was clever, too.

"You must want to know *something* about it," he said.

If he could involve her in his discovery, she would be as guilty as he was himself, and then she would be unable to tell anyone about his find.

"I told you, I don't want to be involved."

"But you are. By keeping my discovery secret, you're already involved."

"How do you know I've kept it secret? How do you know the Secure Division isn't already at your house, searching, taking away your family for questioning?"

A wave of fear swept through his mind and, in a second, his forehead was wet with sweat.

"You haven't, have you?"

"Don't you know what you are risking?" she asked him. "If you're discovered, you could lose your position in the Division, lose your water rights. You'd be placed on minimum rations."

"What am I supposed to do?" he said.

"Give it up! Tell them you've only just found it. No one will know how long you've actually been hiding it."

Give up the bird? Amon recoiled from the idea. It would be killed immediately. And, now that he had seen the trust in its eyes, the way it ceased to struggle as he stroked it, he couldn't let that happen.

"It's a pigeon," he said. "I've identified it."

She seemed to be listening, but said nothing.

"They lived in communities. They weren't wild animals. And people kept them for pleasure. They were called 'homing pigeons' because they always returned home from wherever they were released."

"Let it go if you don't want to report it."

"Let it return *home*? Is that what you're saying? You're saying that it has a home to *go* to?"

Hester stared at him. Her eyes were wide. She looked behind her, checking that no one else had come into the room.

"But there is no 'home' for it to go to, is there, Hester? Ledron is the only surviving community. That's what the Leaders have told us."

"The whole world is a desert," said Hester automatically. "When climate change struck, only the strongest communities survived, only the smartest."

"And then, even *they* began to die," said Amon. It was like reciting a catechism, something they had been taught so often that it was all that they could believe.

"All communication from other isolated settlements stopped more than twenty years ago," Hester said.

Amon looked at her. "And it was only through the knowledge of the Leaders that *our* community kept functioning."

Silence then, while they both looked at the image of the pigeon on the screen.

"That's the way it is," said Hester slowly. "So questioning history is a waste of time."

"It is also heresy," said Amon, "and that is punishable by death."

"Then let the bird go. Release it! Just take it outside tonight, after dark, and let it go!"

"It's injured. It can't fly."

"Then, then . . ." She was beginning to panic.

"I won't harm it," he said. "I won't kill the bird."

"Listen," she hissed, taking a step towards him and bending over so that her face seemed only a few millimetres from his. "You can do what you like, but don't involve me in your plans. You're right, it *is* too late for me to alert the Secure Division. If I was going to do that, I should have done it in the first few minutes after I saw you find the bird. If I say anything now, they'll punish me for not reporting it immediately. But I have plans, plans to move ahead in this community, and I won't have them destroyed by your stupidity and law-breaking."

"To move ahead?" asked Amon.

Hester stood up and looked around the room. For a moment her glance rested on the view from a window, the long, flat stretch of desert that stretched out to a distant horizon.

"I'm sixteen years old. If you think I'm going to dig wells for the rest of my life, you're wrong!"

"But it's the noblest occupation," argued Amon. "All those stories we had in school when we were kids — the ones about the water warriors who dug for water to keep their community alive."

"I don't want to be a hero," she said. "I want to be free — free to use my mind, to make discoveries, to find ways of living in a world that's green."

"On a trickle a day?"

"Once I'm employed as a Future Thinker, I'll have every opportunity to work on inventions, new ideas . . . I can make Ledron a better place. It *has* to be better because what's the point of life in an endless desert with an endless struggle for survival?"

When Amon said nothing, she began again.

"I'm going to be noticed," she said. "My exams are just three weeks away. After that, an invitation to join the Future Division will be just around the corner."

"What about the bird?" Amon asked. "You want to forget that it has to have come from somewhere?"

"I don't know about the bird," she said, burying her head in her hands. "I don't want to think about it. It's too big. Maybe . . . maybe it's . . . I don't know!"

"Maybe there really is another community out there," said Amon.

"Heretic!" said Hester. "Just listen to yourself. Don't rock the boat. Leave these decisions to the Leaders, and, more importantly, don't rock *my* boat. I'm going to make it in this community. I'm going to be somebody and, one day, I'm going to change the way we live! If that means keeping myself squeaky clean, I'm going to do it."

She turned to the door, then spun back round.

"I don't know about the bird," she said. "I never spoke to you about it, and I don't want to speak to you ever again."

She stormed over to the door.

"Listen!" he said. "I'll let it go. I will. I promise. As soon as it can fly, I'll release it. No one will ever know anything about it except you and me."

She looked at him. "*Do* it!" she warned.

The door slammed shut behind her.

Amon turned back to his infoputer and, for some reason, deleted all record of the files he'd been searching that afternoon.

Chapter Four

Chapter Five

The bird, he now knew from his research in the library, would eat almost anything: grain, bread, vegetables, beans. It required nothing that was unavailable. The difficulty would be in smuggling the food, and more water, back to his room from the communal dining hall.

The mealtime siren wailed and Amon set out for the dining room — Lydia must have gone already, she was nowhere to be seen. Inside the building, long lines of tables had been set with cutlery and people were spilling in the doors at the four corners of the room. Amon was required to sit with his Division. As each Division member received the same dinner ration of water, it made dispensing easier.

"Did you get that rash checked out?" asked the Secure Division guard sitting at Amon's table.

"Not yet," said Amon. "It's not bothering me now."

The guard noted the response on his hand-held memory pad. Guards missed nothing. The health and welfare of each member of their Division was their sole occupation.

Marco bounded over the back of his chair and into his seat next to Amon. "That wind is unbelievable!" he said.

"Have you been out in your yacht already?" asked Amon.

"I got quite a few circuits in before the meal siren went. Got a little surprise while I was out there, too."

"What sort of surprise?" asked Amon.

"One of the Leaders was watching me. At least I'm pretty sure he was. He was standing on the viewing platform. I saw him looking at me through his binoculars."

"What's that all about?" asked Amon.

"I'm not sure, yet. Maybe he just likes to watch sailing."

At the front of the room, a marshal was calling for quiet. It was time for the pre-dinner address from one of the Leaders. The lights in the room dimmed and a dark-cloaked figure approached the lit stage. Everyone immediately began clapping. The figure motioned for silence.

There was the usual greeting from the Leaders' Precinct. Then there was a report on the water reserves. They were, as usual, dangerously low, but there was hope that new water discoveries to the south might make a difference. Amon knew what was coming next — the call for a voluntary reduction in water consumption.

"It is only through self-denial that we may succeed in developing a better quality of life for all," began the Leader. "In order to begin work on wells in the south, it is essential that we develop three more Well Divisions. As you all know, Well Division workers cannot work on regular rations. The extra half-litre of water a day for each digger must come from the rations of those who are working in less demanding fields."

Amon saw the heads of several community members bow. They didn't want to hear what was coming next.

"We request that each agricultural worker voluntarily assign fifty mils of their water ration to the new Well Divisions so that work can begin."

Agricultural workers, mainly women and older men, received less water than any other Division. Their work was considered light compared to that of diggers. Lydia was an agricultural worker. She spent her days in the greenhouses, tending seedling vegetable plants. It was hot work. She was always thirsty. How could she be asked to give up even a small portion of her ration?

"Do we have volunteers?" asked the Leader.

It was a clever scheme. Asking for volunteers to come forward at this time, when they were visible in front of the whole community, shamed into action anyone who was reluctant to make the commitment.

"Your community honours you," said the Leader as, one by one, agricultural workers began filing past to sign away a portion of their water ration.

Amon watched his mother move from her seat to the front of the room. She seemed more stooped than usual — tired perhaps. He would have worked on less water himself and given her his, if only there was a way.

As the last person returned to their seat, the Leader smiled down at the assembled community. "Self-sacrifice, hard work, creative conservation," he said. "These are the hallmarks of Ledron. They are the reason why we have survived when all others have failed. Your Leaders admire your courage, your sacrifice, your determination to make Ledron work for the good of all. Go out to your homes and your workplaces in the knowledge that we, your Leaders, are also working for your good night and day. We pledge to work tirelessly for you all."

The room erupted into spontaneous applause. People pushed back their chairs so that they could give a standing ovation.

"Where there is a will, there is water!" he said and, with a flurry of his black cape, he left the stage, flanked by members of the Special Secure Division.

"I'd hate to be working in agriculture," said Marco. "Losing fifty mils a day. That stinks!"

Amon took his plate of food from the Secure Division guard who was passing out the meals. Tonight they were eating wholemeal rolls stuffed with soy rissoles and mung bean sprouts and, because they were well-diggers, there was also a portion of green salad. The vitamin tablets on the edge of the plate were compulsory chewing.

Somehow Amon had to smuggle a small portion of the roll into his clothing to take back to the bird. He ate slowly, chewed steadily, all the time keeping his eyes on the guard, who would eat later, when he could afford to be distracted.

Then, very obviously, he yawned. He did it a second time, more noticeably. "Big day," he said to Marco, loudly enough for the guard to hear. "I'm really tired." He ate a few mouthfuls. Then, while there was still a morsel of bread left in his mouth, he yawned again. At the same time, he put up his hand to cover his mouth and spat into his palm a little of the chewed bread. It stuck against his skin. He laid his hands on his lap and slipped the wet bread up the cuff of his sleeve. The guard hadn't noticed. He ate some more, then risked the same manoeuvre again. It worked a second time. He would collect water for the bird later, when he went to claim his pre-sleep ration.

"Going back out on the track again tonight?" Amon asked Marco.

"Yeah. I want to beat my single circuit record."

"Do you think you'll be entering the July races?" asked Amon.

Marco's brow wrinkled. "Mmm, I hadn't thought about that. Those sailors are so good. I'd be wiped out by them."

"No you wouldn't," coaxed Amon. "You'd be great. You're fearless — and you're fast."

"Huh, you reckon!" For a moment he was quiet. Then he said, "July. That's not long away. I could never be good enough to race by then — could I?"

"What I can't understand," said Amon, "is why we're allowed to sand-yacht." It was something he often thought about. "I mean, what does it contribute to anything?"

"Guess we have to have *some* free time," Marco said, "and something to do in it. I mean, it's not as if a sand yacht uses any fuel or water, and maintenance is virtually nil." He paused for a minute. "I guess I never stopped to think why we get to do it." He laughed. "I don't think about it because I'm too busy enjoying it!"

Chapter Six

Amon left the dining room as soon as he could, pleased to see that Lydia was still sitting at the table, talking with one of her friends. He ran through the alleyways to his home and pushed open the door to the courtyard. In his room, he locked the door behind him and reached under the bed for the bird. It blinked into the light when he lifted off its cover. Amon took it out of the box and sat it on his lap.

He peeled the moist bread from the inside of his sleeve and held it in his hand. "Want some of this?" he offered.

The bird spotted it immediately and stretched its neck forward. Its sharp beak pecked again and again at the bread. It pecked so quickly that Amon thought it might choke. Then it seemed to swallow in one gulp and start on the next piece.

"You must have been starving," he whispered to it, stroking its back.

He stared at it as it sat on his lap. How far had it come? Where had it come *from*? No other community existed. No other community had existed for the last twenty years. That was when communications from other settlements had ceased. If there were still communities existing, then the Leaders would have known about them.

Amon frowned. But the bird *had* to have come from somewhere. So, were the Leaders wrong? That was unthinkable! They couldn't be wrong — about anything. To question their decisions was heresy. There was nothing they didn't know: about water, water conservation, agriculture, education, social organisation . . . It was only thanks to their collective knowledge and decision-making that survival was even possible. They were all-knowing, hard-working and, above all, fair. They possessed no more than any other person in the community, yet their hours of work were longer and their responsibilities far greater than those of any other citizen.

Amon looked at the bird again. He felt his mind was being pulled in different directions. He could not deny what the Leaders had told them — that there was no other life outside the community. The people of Ledron were the last, and yet, here was the bird, sitting on his lap, not a dream, but something solid and real.

He breathed in slowly and deeply. "Hester's right," he said to the bird. "You have to go. You're beautiful, but I can't keep you, can't afford to think about where you came from and what you mean."

He tucked the bird back in the box and slid it under the bed. This animal was making a liar of the Leaders. They could not be wrong, but here it was, evidence of life elsewhere. Amon lay back on his bed. He felt sick. He felt unsafe. He felt strangely insecure in this community that was the only world he knew.

"Amon? Amon, are you in there?"

Lydia was knocking on his door.

"Coming," he called.

He stepped out of his room and into the court-yard. His mother was sitting at the stone table beside the wall. Her face was serious and yet she was smiling at him.

"I'm sorry you had to give up some of your water," he said. "It might not be for long, just until they get the new wells dug and working."

"You shouldn't be sorry," she said. "It's for the good of everyone. How did the dig go today?"

"Good," he told her. "We're on schedule."

He sat down at the table.

"There's a girl in the Division we're working with."

"That's unusual," said Lydia. "She's got to be strong."

"And clever."

Lydia raised her eyebrows.

"I don't *like* her," said Amon. "I was just talking to her, that's all."

"You don't have enough friends," said Lydia.

"I've got Marco," said Amon, "and you."

Lydia looked down. Her shoulders sagged. To Amon it seemed that something had sucked the breath from her.

"What's wrong, Mum?" he asked.

She tried to look up but couldn't.

"Mum?"

Beyond the courtyard, footsteps tripped along the cobbled lane.

"Come inside," she told him. "I don't want to talk here."

The small room that was half Lydia's bed space and half living area was lit with a pale light. Wind generation provided each home with two hours of illumination after dark.

Amon looked around and, as always, took pleasure in the colours of the room. Lydia loved colour. Coloured cloths hung at the windows, a bright red and green cotton rug lay over her bed. She had painted bright borders of flowers along the tops of the walls and patterns of colour dotted the stone floor.

"I love this place," she said, as they came inside and sat down — Lydia on her bed and Amon in a chair beside her. She looked up at the walls. "I wish we could have real flowers, the water to grow them and water so that we could bring them into the house in containers."

"At least you work with plants," said Amon, trying to cheer her up.

"Boxes of corn seedlings!" she said with a laugh. "There's not a lot of pleasure in that. I want lilies and roses and, in spring, daffodils and bluebells and tulips."

"You spend too much time in the library, looking at the way the world *was*," said Amon.

"I don't remember flowers," said Lydia. "But I remember my mother talking about them. She grew them when she was a child. They had a garden with a stream running through it."

Lydia stared into space. "And then the world began to dry up."

"Why do you think the rains stopped?" asked Amon. He had, of course, studied the subject in school, but there had been so many theories and no one was sure which one was correct.

"I don't know," said Lydia, "and, in the end, it didn't matter. What mattered was that the climate had changed and the world was at war. Country fought country for water supplies and all the while the lakes dried up and the rivers disappeared."

"Your father held out longer than most, didn't he?" Amon had asked the same question many times, but he wanted to hear the story again.

Lydia nodded. "He was smart. He realised that he could no longer farm as he had, in one fixed place. He became a nomad, with just a herd of sheep and goats, a tent and a horse each for the three of us to ride. We lived like that for more than five years, but each year it became harder and harder to find water. Each little oasis or spring that we came to know eventually dried up."

"And that's when you heard about Ledron?"

"Yes. We met other nomads who were heading here, and refugees from the last water wars in the north. We travelled together for weeks, and when we arrived, they took us in."

Amon watched her.

"I was very young, but even so I knew it was different," she said. "There were so many rules, so many restrictions. We were used to freedom, to making decisions for ourselves and, suddenly, if we wanted to survive, we had to obey and not question."

"But it worked?"

"In a way, yes. There was no personal freedom. Work was hard, as it is now. But we received enough water and food and that was more than we'd had in the desert."

"And now we're all there is."

"The last community," said Lydia. "Our Leaders knew what they were doing. They know what they're doing now, even if . . ." She stopped and her head dropped so that she was looking into the palms of her hands. "Even if it seems so hard at times."

"What did you want to talk to me about?" asked Amon. He wanted to go for water for himself and the bird.

She looked up at him and he saw that she was crying.

"Amon. Amon." She said his name as though all she wanted was to hear it.

"Mum? What's wrong?"

"I don't ever want to leave you," she said, and she was crying again.

Amon shifted across to sit beside her. He put his arm around her shoulders and pulled her close to him.

"Are you sick?"

She pulled herself up straight. "I've . . . I've found a lump," she said, her lip trembling. "Under my arm."

Amon's stomach lurched.

"I found it a few weeks ago when I was cleaning myself after work. It's small, but not too small. It's in my armpit."

"What does it mean?"

"I'm not totally sure. I can't be, without going to the Medical Centre — and I don't want to do that. Not yet."

"Can you still work?"

"I'm fine. At least, I think I am. Today, when I was lifting boxes of seedlings, I thought I was losing strength in the arm with the lump. And tonight, I think there's some swelling in my upper arm."

"Have you checked in the library for any information?"

"Of course."

"And? What have you found out?"

"Amon." She held him tight. "I'm sure it's cancer."

The word burned him. His mouth felt cold and dry.

"You don't know, Mum. It could be anything."

"My mother had the same thing," said Lydia.

"Then, how long, I mean, what's going to happen? Mum? What do we do?"

"All I can think of is that I want to live long enough to see you grow up. That's my dream."

"You will — won't you?"

"Amon, in a world with water, in a world that could spare labour to nurse very sick people, I might live for a few more years, perhaps quite a few more. But not here. You know that. As soon as

I can't work, can't contribute, I'm a liability. I've no right to take another's labour just so that I can stay alive."

"But I don't want you to . . . to be retired. I want you to live for as long as you can. I'll look after you. You can have my water and food."

"Amon, you know that's impossible."

"It's not fair! It's not fair!"

He stood up. He wanted to throw something. To shout. To scream. He felt so powerless to do anything that might help.

"Don't tell *any*one," he said. "Don't even tell your friends, Mum. We have to keep this to ourselves. We have to think what to do."

Lydia was nodding. She was looking at him as though she was the child and he was the one in charge.

"I'll think of something, Mum. I will. Don't go to the Medical Centre. Please don't."

"No," said Lydia. "I won't do anything without talking to you. We'll wait. Perhaps the lump will go away."

He looked at her for a moment. "I have to go for water," he said. "I'll be back soon. Remember what I said, Mum. Don't tell *any*one!"

Chapter Seven

Marco was leaning on the water dispenser, staring into the distance, when Amon arrived to claim his night ration.

"What's up?" Marco asked as Amon gently shoved him aside.

"Huh?"

"You look worried."

"Do I? Nah, I'm good."

"You know," said Marco, sitting down on a seat nearby, "you never told me that your father was an engineer — that he worked in sand-yacht design."

"I didn't know him."

"How old were you when he died?"

"He didn't 'die'. He was retired."

Marco nodded. "Yeah, I know. I'm sorry."

"I don't remember him. I was just a baby."

"He was responsible for developing the P-class racer," said Marco. "That machine was revolutionary. He was on the brink of inventing something even better. Did you know that?"

Amon nodded his head.

"Some people say he was developing a new material that would mean bearings wouldn't need replacing until yachts had sailed for hundreds, maybe thousands of kilometres. With that sort of technology, we could begin exploring, maybe find new water reserves."

"Yeah, well, he didn't get to make that discovery, did he? How come you know this stuff, anyway?"

Marco drummed a finger on the top of the water dispenser.

"This evening I was talking to one of the old guys who sail. He was raving on about the P-class. Reckons there's never been anything to better it. Reckons your father was a genius."

"Huh," said Amon. He entered his code and filled his cup from the dispenser, then waited for Marco to go. He couldn't drink his water and hold back a mouthful for the bird until he was alone. But Marco was in the mood for talking.

"I found out some stuff about Hester. She's

that girl you're interested in," he grinned.

"I'm not interested in any girl," mumbled Amon.

"I don't like your chances," said Marco, ignoring him. "She's a couple of years older than you."

Marco waited for some reaction, but Amon didn't respond.

"She's smart," he said. "I was talking to Rylo, this guy I sail with sometimes. He was in her class at East-side School. He says she topped all the exams. She also outdid everyone else in the gym, including the guys."

Amon shrugged.

"But listen to this," said Marco. "She and I have something in common."

Amon waited for him to continue.

"She was brought up in an orphanage, just like me," said Marco. "Her parents both died in a well collapse when she was a baby."

"That's too bad," said Amon. He wished Marco would finish whatever he had to say and go.

"Rylo said he wouldn't ever want to get in her way."

"What does that mean?"

"It means she's got ambitions. Reckons she's

going all the way to the top. Says she wants to be an adviser to the Leaders."

"Listen, I've got to get back," said Amon. "My mum's waiting for me."

"You're lucky," said Marco. "You're lucky you've got a mum to care about."

"I know," said Amon. He swallowed, and felt a hard lump in his throat.

"I gotta go, too," said Marco. "You know, Amon, you really should think about sailing with me. I could easily give you some lessons. We could take out a learner's yacht. There's no way you'd ever go fast enough on that to do yourself any harm."

Amon shook his head. "Nah, not me."

"Suit yourself," said Marco. He aimed a play punch at Amon's shoulder. "You don't know what you're missing," he said.

Back in his room, Amon let the water trickle from his mouth into the cup, then offered it to the bird. It drank until the cup was dry.

Amon stroked its feathers as it lay contentedly in the cradle of his arm. He felt under its wing and discovered softer, fluffier feathers. The bird was warm. Gently, Amon stretched out its wing. It was like a jointed fan and the wing feathers were longer and stronger than those on the rest of its body. He tried to imagine the bird in the air, with its wings spread in flight, as he'd seen in images on the library encyclopaedia. To fly would be to be free, but free to go where?

"Where did you come from?" he whispered to the animal. "Why can't you talk to me, bird?"

Later, when Amon went to see Lydia, she was already in bed, her white cotton sheets pulled up to her chin as if she was hiding.

"Had your drink?" she asked.

"Yes."

Beside her bed was a framed photo. It was of Amon's father, a clean-shaven man holding a tiny baby. Amon picked up the frame.

"I wish he was still here," said Lydia, looking at Amon. "I always wish that but, now. . ." She paused and took a deep breath. "Now I wish it more than ever."

"You didn't know he was going to be retired, did you, Mum?" asked Amon.

Lydia shook her head. "No."

"You didn't even know he was sick."

"That's right. He kept it from me."

"But why?"

"I don't know. We shared everything. I suppose
. . . I suppose he was trying to protect me from
the sadness."

"So, one day he just didn't come home?"

"That's exactly what happened." Lydia reached
out for the frame. Amon passed it to her and sat
down on the edge of the bed where they could
both see it.

"He could do anything, but his passion was
the yachts. Not so much sailing them — he wasn't
actually very good at that — but he liked designing
and building them. He was always looking for the
perfect machine."

They sat in silence for a minute.

"The night he didn't come home, well, at first I
didn't really worry. He'd been spending more and
more time down at the yacht house, dropping in
after work, so I thought he'd just forgotten about
the evening meal. And then, just as the meal siren
went off and I was getting ready to take you to the
dining hall, someone from the Secure Division
knocked on the door."

"And that was the first you knew?"

Lydia ran her thumb up and down the edge of the frame.

"They said he had a heart complaint, that he'd been to the Medical Centre with chest pains several times over a period of two or three months. He hadn't told me about that. In the end, the doctors told him that he was no longer fit to work."

"But he must have known that he was going to be retired. And he didn't even say goodbye to us. Why didn't he, Mum?"

"I don't know. Maybe it was too hard for him."

"And you never got to see his body?"

"No. They said it was what he wanted. To be buried before the news was given to me."

Amon sat still. It was so quiet in the room that it was possible to hear the dust driving against the outside of the door. How quiet would it be when his mother was gone, too?

"I used to think he'd come back," said Lydia. "Sometimes, at night, I thought he would walk back in the door — that his going away was just a bad dream."

Amon took the frame and returned it to the table.

"I don't want to leave you, Amon," she said.

"Not before I have to. I don't want to be retired."

"That's not going to happen, Mum," he promised. "It's not."

Chapter Eight

A week after Lydia told Amon about the lump in her armpit, the bird was still unable to fly. When Amon lifted it from its box, it only fluttered across the floor on its belly. Its injured leg was slow to heal, and the bird seemed to be losing strength.

With the door to his room locked, Amon sat on the bed with the creature on his lap. He tipped the bird on to its back. It struggled for a moment, then lay still, as if it understood what must be done. Carefully, he smoothed back its feathers to expose its leg. The wound was weeping — a scab had still not formed over the tear. Around the edges of the injury, the skin was swollen, tight, and blue. Amon pressed the area gently, and the bird struggled.

"It's infected," he said quietly. "That's why you're not improving."

He lifted the animal back into its box. What he needed was an antibiotic, a tablet that he could crush and feed to the animal. Or better still, some antibiotic powder — the sort that was prescribed by the Medical Centre if anyone cut or grazed themselves while on a dig.

Suddenly, he knew what had to be done. He winced at the thought, but there was nothing else for it.

He took down a box of unusual rocks that he'd discovered while on well-digs and chose the sharpest one. Then he pulled up the leg of his pants and held the rock edge against his shin, closed his eyes and ground it into his leg. The pain was horrible. His eyes stung and his brow was instantly covered in sweat. He looked down at the raw graze and breathed in and out, deeply, until the pain slowly dulled. Then he rolled down the leg of his pants and went out into the courtyard.

"Where are you going?" asked Lydia.

"I should have told you earlier, Mum. I grazed my leg on the dig today. I should have gone to the Medical Centre as soon as I got back."

"Let me see it," said Lydia, but Amon had already hurried out the gate.

"I'll be back soon," he called.

At the centre, the nurse questioned him about not reporting the injury as soon as it happened.

"I just wanted to keep digging," he said. "It didn't feel too bad until I cleaned it just now. Then it started bleeding again."

"I'm giving you some antibiotic powder," she said. "Puff it onto the wound twice a day. Come and see me if it doesn't clear up in three to four days."

Amon nodded. It had been so easy.

He was just leaving the centre when Marco appeared in the alleyway outside.

"What's up?" he asked.

"Nothing much," shrugged Amon. "Grazed my leg on some rocks today when we were digging. Had to get it looked at."

"You weren't digging today. You were on the winch."

Amon felt his face grow red.

"I didn't actually mean when I was digging. It was on the way home. We were horsing around and Pele gave me a shove. I landed on some sharp rocks."

Amon knew Marco didn't believe him.

"You know how I said I thought one of the

Leaders was watching me the other day when I was out sailing?" said Marco, leaning against the wall of the Medical Centre.

"Yeah."

"Well, I was right."

"What's it all about?"

"I'm not sure yet. But, when I took my yacht back to the yacht house this afternoon, one of the wind turbine mechanics was waiting for me. He asked if I wanted him to take a look at my yacht. Wanted to know if I needed any work done on it."

"And do you?"

"*Do* I!" Marco raised his eyebrows. "That old crate practically needs rebuilding, only I never have time to look at it. I mean, I figure I can either use the little spare time I have to sail, or I can spend it repairing the yacht."

"And you want to sail."

"Sure do. But now, for some strange reason, this mechanic is going to work on the yacht *for* me."

"Did you ask him why?"

"Of course, but all he said was that he'd been given instructions to help me out."

"Weird."

"I know. It'd be kind of spooky if it wasn't so good. Just think, a yacht that's working properly might actually do what I want it to!"

"Does that mean you're going to enter the races that are coming up?"

Marco looked into the distance. Then he smiled to himself and slapped Amon on the shoulder. "Yeah! I reckon it does. That trophy for the sixteen-year-olds — it could be mine if I have a yacht that goes, and if I keep practising."

Marco began wandering off in the direction of the hostel where he lived. Amon watched him go and wondered, not for the first time, what it must be like to live alone, without a mother or father. Then he thought of his own mother and a wave of something heavy swept over him. For the last few days, they'd said nothing more of her illness. It had been almost possible to pretend that she had never told him about finding the lump.

Amon kicked at the dusty ground, gripped the antibiotic powder tightly in his hand and headed for home.

Lydia was inside when he got back. He stepped lightly into the courtyard so that she wouldn't know he had returned. In his room, he reached under the bed for the bird. It huddled in a corner of its box and he thought again how utterly strange it was to have something so alive and yet so completely foreign in his possession.

When the bird was on his lap, he tipped it on to its back and pushed aside its feathers. Exposing the wound, he puffed a little of the yellow powder on to it.

"This might help," he said to it softly. "It might make you better, and then, you have to go."

Go *where*? asked a voice in his head.

The bird lay calmly on his lap. Amon stroked it. He felt the rough skin on its uninjured leg and the soft, fluffy feathers that grew closer to its body. They were so light and delicate. He ran his fingers through them and felt the top of the bird's leg where it connected with its body. Then, with a start, he realised that he was touching something that wasn't skin or feathers. It was a small, hard object.

He parted the bird's feathers quickly and found that he was staring down at a tiny metal band fixed to the creature's upper leg. Amon's heart beat fast. This was nothing natural. It was something that had been constructed and deliberately placed there. He swallowed hard and, though he knew the door to his room was locked, he looked behind him to check.

The band was only a few millimetres wide. It had been moulded around the bird's leg and pressed closed. If he could prise it open and take it off, he'd be able to study it more closely.

He reached out to the drawers beside his bed and took out a pair of nail scissors.

"Don't move," he whispered to the bird.

Very carefully, so that there was no chance of the scissors slipping and injuring the animal further, he slid an open blade under the join of the band. The metal was soft and pliable. He placed the scissors on the bed and reached back to pull apart the two ends of the strip.

The bird moved. Amon placed the band on top of the drawers while he returned the creature to its box and slid it under the bed.

When he picked up the band again, what he saw made his mind spin. Engraved into the metal were five tiny letters: OASIS. He looked again

Chapter Eight

towards the door. His eyes roamed the room as if searching for an escape route.

Five tiny letters on a band of metal. Five letters that changed everything. To accept that the bird had come from another place, a place where animal life somehow still managed to exist, was a huge step. Now, Amon was forced to accept something else: wherever the bird had come from, human life existed also. Someone had engraved those letters on the band. Someone from another place.

"Amon!"

It was Lydia. Her voice was pitched high. She sounded afraid.

"Amon?" She rattled the handle of his door. "Why have you got your door locked?"

"Coming, Mum."

He picked up the band and dropped it into the top drawer.

"What's up?"

Lydia's feet were bare. She was wearing her singlet top. She stepped inside and shut the door behind her. He could see the panic in her eyes.

"Amon, look!" She stretched out her arms towards him. "Look!"

"I can't see anything — I don't know what I'm

supposed to be looking at."

"This arm," she said, holding it out further than the other. "Can't you see the swelling?"

Amon looked from one limb to the other. It was barely noticeable, but she was right. The upper left arm was very slightly larger than the right.

"It's puffy," she said. "It's so much bigger than the other. Oh, Amon, they'll notice! They'll send me to the Medical Centre. They'll do tests and then they'll find out and then . . ."

"Stop! Stop it, Mum!" He took her hands and gently pushed her on to the bed. "Sit down. Take some deep breaths."

"But . . ."

"Mum, it's not noticeable. It's not as bad as you think. No one else would be able to tell."

"Do you think so?"

"Yes."

"But if it keeps getting bigger then . . ."

He sat down beside her and put his arm around her shoulders. It felt so strange that, of the two of them, it should be him taking care of her.

"Mum, I told you. It's going to be all right. But you mustn't tell anyone but me about your arm or the lump. No matter how much you want to tell a friend, it has to be our secret. The more time we have, the better we can plan what to do."

Lydia nodded silently. "Okay, okay. I was panicking. I can see that now. You can't really tell there's any swelling, can you? Not unless you know to look for it."

She was pleading with him to agree.

"That's right," said Amon reassuringly. "No one can tell."

"So I just go back to bed."

"Yes. And try to go to sleep."

Lydia stood up and moved towards the door.

"I don't want to think about the future," she said, as she was about to go out. "I . . . I *can't*."

"You don't have to," said Amon. "That will be my job.

Chapter Nine

In the weeks that followed, the bird grew stronger, and a shallow, grey scab grew across the jagged tear on its injured leg. At night, when Lydia had gone to bed, Amon would take the creature from its box and allow it to flutter from the top of his drawers to his bed.

Sometimes, it stood in one place, stretched out its wings and flapped them, as if exercising its muscles. Then it would shake itself until its feathers stood out at all angles.

One night, as Amon watched it, it began to preen itself, its neck twisting this way and that as it ran each feather in turn through its beak. Its coat grew shiny. The bloodstains from its wound began to fade, and then, one evening, it made a strange sound.

Amon had been lying on his bed watching

it. He sat up when he heard the soft cooing, and stared at it. The sound was a low, reverberating rumble, like none he had ever heard before.

"What do you want?" he asked the bird. "Do you want to leave? Do you want to go back to wherever it is you came from?"

The bird made the sound again — twice— and flapped its wings.

"Soon," promised Amon. "When I know you're strong enough to fly."

He flopped back on to his bed and closed his eyes. Something that had been nagging at the back of his mind for days was stirring to the surface, and he didn't want to face it. He rolled over on to his front and buried his head in his pillow.

The swelling in Lydia's arm had not reduced. It was only slightly larger, and still unnoticeable to anyone who was not looking for it, but it was not improving. Amon had tried to think of a way to avoid what might soon happen, and, over and over again, his mind had returned to the bird.

It had come from some other place — a place where there were people. Perhaps they were people who would know how to make Lydia well, who would have the time and the medicine to help her. It was a wild dream, he knew that, but there *was* no other hope — not here, in Ledron, where nothing but your own labour secured your right to live.

Amon rolled on to his back again and lay with his hands under his head, staring up at the ceiling. He tried to imagine a community where even the very ill were cared for, where people grew old and died when they were ready to die. A community where there was enough water, even for animals.

He looked across at the bird. He was no longer convinced that these things were impossible. Now that the bird was here, anything was possible.

As far as Amon knew, no one had ever tried to leave Ledron. No one with any sense would ever entertain the idea. To walk away into the desert without food or water was to die, and why would anyone choose to do it when everyone accepted that there *was* no place to go?

But now Amon knew differently. Somewhere, there *was* another place, and if there was a way to travel great distances in a short time, to fly like a bird so that you could explore and search, perhaps he might find it. Perhaps he and Lydia might find it together.

An idea began to form in Amon's mind. It did not arrive suddenly, like a magic, instant solution. Rather, it drifted slowly into his consciousness, like a blurred picture coming into focus. First he sensed movement, then he pictured a trail of dust. He closed his eyes. He was standing at the edge of the racing circuit and the dust was coming from the rear wheels of Marco's sand yacht, the old one that the mechanic had repaired. The wind was strong and it was filling the red and yellow sail of the yacht so that the craft was sucked along at great speed.

Amon sat up. How fast could a yacht travel? How far? Could it cover a hundred kilometres? Two hundred, *three*? He looked over at the bird. How far had *it* come?

That night, in his sleep, Amon's mind raced. In his dreams, the wind rushed against his face. A bright sail, tight and shining in the sun, stretched above him and, sitting beside him in the sand yacht, Lydia stared ahead with hope in her eyes.

Amon woke early, before it was completely

light. A strange wind was blowing around the house and it was uncomfortably hot in his room. He slid out of bed and opened the window above his desk. As he listened to it, the wind seemed to grow stronger.

Under the bed, the bird was moving restlessly in its box. Amon reached for it and pulled the container into the centre of the floor.

"What's the problem?" he said, taking off the lid and crooning to the animal in the grey light.

The bird hopped onto the edge of the box and stretched its wings. It tilted its head this way and that. It seemed brighter than usual, more alert.

A sudden gust of wind howled around the house. Amon looked up as the curtains at the open window blew about. From the corner of his eye, he saw something move from the floor. The bird was flying across the room. Before Amon had time to stand up, it was on the window ledge. A moment later, it had spread its wings and disappeared out the open window and into the early-morning darkness.

Amon rushed to the window. The bird was sitting on the courtyard wall. He looked about. There was no one in sight. As he watched, the bird also looked around. Then, suddenly, it launched itself off the wall, flew in a circle above the house, and was gone.

Amon stared down at the empty box lying in the middle of the floor. It was over. His time with the bird had come to an end. No goodbye. Nothing. He had cared for it, willed it to live and be well, but it had left him. He felt empty and alone, as though the bird, or perhaps he, himself, had died.

"Amon?"

Lydia was tapping on his door, as she did at the same time every work morning.

"Time to get up, love."

"Coming," he mumbled.

He closed the box and pushed it back under the bed.

Chapter Ten

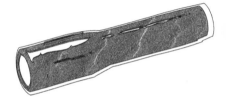

"I want to learn to sail."

Marco, rigging his yacht, looked up. Amon was leaning against the railing that edged the yachting circuit. Two other craft were already out on the track.

"You? *You* want to learn?"

"Yup."

Marco tied a figure of eight knot in the mainsheet he had just finished threading along the boom.

"*You* want to sail a *yacht*?"

Amon nodded. "Don't you think I can do it?"

Marco let the end of the mainsheet drop and stood up. "I didn't say that. I'm just surprised, that's all."

"Do you have time — to teach me, I mean?"

"Sure. Of course I do."

"I won't get in the way of your racing practice?"

"No. There's nothing much involved. I just show you a few basics to get you started, and then it's up to you. The best way to learn is from your own mistakes."

"When can we start?"

Marco looked over to the yacht house. "I think there's a beginner's model free now. The girl who booked it hasn't shown up."

"Suits me."

Marco hitched his yacht to a railing post and led the way.

"Just one thing," he said to Amon, when they were almost there.

"What's that?"

"I thought you were, you know, scared to sail, after you saw that guy get dragged years ago?"

"Yeah, well, I changed my mind. I figure it's time I learned to have some fun, and sailing's about the only option."

Amon didn't like lying to Marco and he didn't like thinking about why he wanted to sail. If he stopped to analyse what he was planning, it seemed so impossible, completely crazy and unreal, that he might as well give up before he started.

But it was more than two weeks since the bird had left and, for every minute of every day since then, Amon had thought about it — not just about the bird, but about where it had come from. There was no hope for Lydia here. When other people began to notice she wasn't well . . . he willed the thought to go from his mind. But, if there was another place, another community where he could find help for her, where at the very least, she could live as long as she was able, then he *had* to locate it. When they would go, how they would manage to get there, if they would find help when and if they arrived, these were questions he could not yet answer. All he knew for certain was that their only way of leaving Ledron was by yacht, and, to do that, he must first learn to sail.

"This is the one," said Marco, leaning over a small, one-person yacht at the back of the building. He went to a desk and entered something into the computer. "Right, we're all ready. It's yours for a couple of hours. I'll just make a few checks on it. Make sure it's shipshape."

Marco took some tools out of the pocket of his jacket and bent over the yacht. He began checking and tightening bolts.

"You know that girl in the Well Division?" he said as he worked.

"Hester?" asked Amon.

"Yeah."

"What about her?"

"She's gone to work for the Future Thinkers."

"I wondered what had happened to her. She hasn't been on the digs for three weeks now. How did you hear?" asked Amon.

Marco dropped his tools on to the ground and walked over to the workbench to collect a can of lubricant. He squirted a few drops around the hub of the wheels.

"She told me."

"When were you talking to her?"

"Actually, I've been talking to her quite a lot lately." He looked over at Amon and grinned.

"Are you two, like . . ."

"Going out together? Yeah, I guess you could say that."

For a moment, Amon wondered if she had said anything to Marco about the bird. Then he remembered that there was no way Hester would risk her own chances of promotion by doing that.

"She's cool," said Marco. "I mean, she's really

tough — she knows what she wants to do with her future and stuff, but she's really . . ."

"Really what?" asked Amon.

"Good. She's a good person. She wants to help people, wants to make things better. She keeps saying that there's got to be a better way to live than to just work for water."

"Everyone knows that. It's just that we don't have a choice."

"I know, but she has this dream that we can change it. She has these amazing ideas, and, now that she's working with Future Thinkers, she's going to make them happen."

"Does she sail?"

Marco laughed. "I didn't say she was perfect! She's a natural, but she's got a lot to learn. I've started giving her some lessons." He returned the lubricant to the workbench and picked up his tools again.

"Push the cart on to the track," he instructed Amon. "I'll carry the mast and sail. And I'll grab some safety gear."

The yacht was light, with a small bucket seat that barely seemed to clear the ground.

"How many can you fit in your machine?"

"Two," Marco told him. "Okay, ready to rig her?"

Under Marco's instruction, Amon threaded the blue and white sail on to the mast, fixed it to the boom and slotted the mast into a hole at the front of the craft.

"Look out!" warned Marco as the wind caught the sail and spun it round.

Amon ducked just in time.

"Now I'll show you how to use the mainsheet."

"I can never understand why a rope is called a mainsheet!" said Amon with a laugh. "It sounds more like a sail."

Marco licked his finger and held it up in the air. "Do this," he said to Amon. "Now, which way is the wind coming from?"

Amon took a guess.

"Dead right," said Marco. "So, you can sail *with* the wind and you can sail *across* it. The only direction you can't sail is *into* it."

Amon nodded.

"Here," said Marco, passing a helmet and gloves to Amon. "Put these on. You should probably have elbow and shin pads, but there's only a breeze blowing today. You're not going to be going anywhere fast."

"Right," Amon said when he was wearing the gear. "Do I get in?"

"Get in and buckle up."

"Where are the brakes?"

"There aren't any."

"What!"

"Relax. I'll show you how to stop."

Amon didn't feel like relaxing. He felt scared stiff. "What if it just takes off and . . ."

"I said, I'll show you."

For the next half-hour, Marco instructed him on how to steer with the foot pedals, how to tighten the mainsheet and how to let it out to slow the yacht down.

"And you stop by turning back into the wind," he said.

"You make it sound easy," Amon said nervously. His hands were shaking.

"It's not that hard," Marco assured him. "Are you ready to make this machine move? I'll run alongside you."

By the end of the lesson, Amon was exhausted, but he had taken the first steps towards sailing. He could make the yacht move and he could make it stop. With some serious concentration, he could also steer it in a pretty straight line.

"You're a natural!" Marco said as they pushed the craft back into the yacht house.

Amon laughed nervously. "I don't think so and I've taken up half of your sailing slot."

"That's okay," Marco reassured him. "Tomorrow you're on your own. From now on, you get better by practising. I'll be around if you want to ask anything, but, basically, it's just you, the yacht and the wind."

For the next two weeks, Amon went out in the yacht every evening. Lydia seemed pleased that he had an interest other than going to the library.

"It's our day off tomorrow," she said one night as they were going to bed. "Why don't I come out to the circuit in the afternoon and watch you sail?"

"Sure," agreed Amon. "That would be great."

Lydia smiled at him. Then she gave him a tight hug. Neither of them said anything about her arm.

Amon went to his room. The community lights had just been turned off, but he was used to finding his way in the dark. He pulled back the covers of his bed and lay down. The window above the desk was open, but the night was warm. Moonlight played across the curtains. The sky was covered in bright stars. Amon closed his eyes. His breathing grew deep and rhythmical. He felt himself dissolving into sleep. Then suddenly, he was wide awake. His eyes were open and he could hear a faint scratching. He had heard that noise before. He turned his head to the window, and there it was — the bird.

It was pacing back and forth along the ledge. Amon held his breath. Would it stay or go? As he watched, it spread its wings and flew down on to the end of his bed, a pale shape in the darkness. Amon tried not to move. The bird turned around twice, then cooed softy. Quietly, Amon slipped out of bed and shut the window.

"What are you doing here, bird?" he whispered to the animal.

He crossed the floor on tiptoe and slowly reached out to it. It was so sleek and smooth. He stroked it and it didn't move away.

"Bird," said Amon. He felt like crying. It was so wonderful to have it back — and so dangerous.

Amon sat down, lifted the creature on to his

lap and felt for its injured leg. The skin from the wound had healed, but it was still rough. He ran his fingers up the leg to where it joined the animal's body. It was too much to hope for — but there it was, something small and hard. Another metal band! His stomach churned with excitement. He felt the other leg and, once again, touched metal. There was not one, but *two* slim metal bands attached to the creature.

Amon possessed a small battery-powered light. Everyone had one, although they were to be used only in cases of extreme emergency. With the bird under his arm, he closed the curtains and took the light and a pair of scissors from his drawer. He sat back on the bed and tipped the bird over. Using the emergency light to see, he carefully prised the bands off the bird's legs. Then he placed the creature back on the bed.

He was shaking as he straightened out the thin metal loops and turned them over in his hand. He shone the light on to the first — and saw a minute engraving. He reached for his magnifying glass. "Two, nine, four, three, five, eight," he read aloud. He held the magnifying lens over the second band. A single word gleamed up at him: "freedom".

Amon's whole body tingled. He felt alert, tense, ready for action — but *what* action? He looked down at the bird.

"Thank you," he breathed. "Thank you, thank you." He laid his head close to the animal. It didn't stir. "You sleep," he whispered to it. "Who knows how far you've come."

Chapter Ten

Chapter Eleven

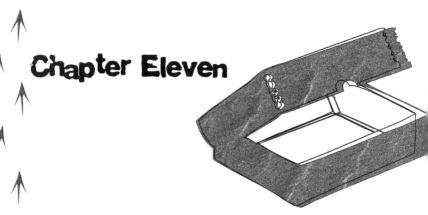

Very early next morning, before it was light, Amon woke to a tapping on his door. He blinked his eyes open, felt the weight of the bird on his feet, and was sure he had been asleep only minutes. When he looked at his watch, he saw that it was just after 5 am. It was too early for Lydia to be calling him.

"Who is it?" he asked quietly.

The tapping came again.

The bird was also awake. It held its head on one side, listening. Amon picked his jacket off the floor, scooped the bird into it and pushed it under the bed.

"Who is it?" he asked again when he was standing at the door.

"It's me, Hester. Let me in. It's urgent. Hurry!"

"What do you want?"

"Let me in! I don't want to be seen."

He opened the door and she pushed past him into the room.

"What are you doing here?" he asked, closing the door behind her.

"You kept it!" she accused. "You said you'd release it. You promised!" Her eyes were wild and desperate. "You promised — and you lied!"

"I didn't lie. I did what I said I would."

"I'm not stupid, Amon. It's here. It's been seen."

"How do you know?"

"So, you *do* still have it."

"I do, but I released it, honestly, I promise."

"Then how . . . ?"

"It came back, last night. My window was open and it just . . . arrived."

He could see that she doubted him.

"It's been seen," she repeated bluntly.

"How do you know?"

She didn't reply.

"You're with the Future Division now, aren't you? Marco told me."

She nodded. "I went back to my lab about an hour ago. When I switched on my computer, an alert was waiting for me."

"You work in the middle of the *night*?"

"Sometimes it's the most productive time for thinking."

"And this alert — it actually said that the bird had been seen?"

"No, it said that there was an emergency and that there was to be a search at six o'clock."

"So how do you know it's anything to do with the bird?"

"I can't tell you that. But you have to trust me. No matter what reason is given for the search, the bird is what the Secure Division will be looking for."

"Why are you telling me this? Why do you care what happens to me?"

"I care because we're in this together. Like it or not, I'm part of what happened all those weeks ago when you first found the bird — when I should have reported you and I didn't."

"You're lying," he said slowly. "You know something else."

"What are you talking about?"

"You've risked everything coming here. What if you were seen? It would have been far safer for you to have kept out of this, to have hoped that if I *was* found out, I wouldn't mention that you had anything to do with the bird."

"Look, if the bird's here, if it's still with you, you're going to have to do some fast thinking."

"You'd better go, before it gets any lighter," said Amon.

"You'll let it go?"

"I'll deal with it," he said.

She reached for the door handle and turned it silently.

"Hester? Thanks."

When she had gone, Amon reached under the bed for the bird. There was no way he could release it before it had been given food and water.

He let himself into the courtyard. The sun was just rising and a cold, red glow spread out towards him from the horizon. He walked to the far wall, crouched down and marched his fingers along the mortar between two rocks. A section of the hard line of cement moved. He picked it out with his fingernails and laid it on the ground. He did the same on a second edge of the rock, then the third and the fourth. Now that the rock was loose, he slipped his fingers into the grooves where the cement had been and lifted it out.

Amon worked fast. The stone wall was hollow.

For strength, it had been constructed as two walls that tapered towards the top and leaned together where the capping stones were placed. Amon had watched the builders make it when he was just eight. He had enjoyed using a knife to loosen the cement before it hardened, creating a secret hiding place for his toys. Now it would have a far more important use.

He went back into his room and put the bird into the box he had kept it in when he first found it. Then he carried the box to the wall, inserted it into the cavity, replaced the rock and the mortar and went back to his room. Suddenly, he remembered the leg bands. He scooped them out of the drawer and looked desperately around the room. His eyes settled on the curtains. The narrow hem along the bottom was open at each end. He pushed the bands into it. It was five minutes to six. Lydia was due to wake him in ten minutes, but an emergency siren was already wailing over the sleeping community.

"Who would take water without permission?" Lydia asked Amon, when the guards had gone.

"Why would someone do such a thing?"

Amon shrugged. They were standing in the courtyard, waiting for the all-clear siren to sound. The guards had been methodical in their search: stripping beds, emptying the contents from drawers and cupboards, conducting swift body searches. Now, from neighbouring houses, came the noise of people putting things back the way they had been.

"I mean, you're only stealing from someone else," continued Lydia. "There *is* only so much water to go round."

So we're told, thought Amon. Just as we're told we're the last community to exist. Just as we were told it was stolen water that the Secure Division was searching for. Just as we're told, he thought bitterly, that, when someone is sick or old, there aren't the resources to care for them.

"Are you still going yachting today?" asked Lydia, changing the subject.

"Doesn't look like there's going to be any wind," said Amon, looking at the sky.

"Well, I'm going to stitch," announced Lydia. "Embroider."

"I didn't know you could do that sort of thing."

"Oh, yes," said Lydia. "I used to do it when you were little. I sewed flowers on to your cotton gowns."

"What are you going to stitch now?"

Lydia looked around the courtyard. "I'm going to embroider a garden," she said. "With flowers in it. I'm . . ." She hung her head and studied the ground. "I'm going to embroider you and I, standing among them." Her voice shook.

"Mum, don't cry," said Amon. He put his arms around her. "Please don't cry."

Lydia choked back a sob. "I feel tired," she said. "I feel tired all the time. Sometimes, at work, I feel too tired to lift the boxes of seedlings."

"Why didn't you tell me?"

"Please don't let them take me away, Amon. Please don't let them."

"It's going to be all right, Mum. It really is, I promise."

ChapterTwelve

All morning, Amon worried about the bird. He hated to think of it in the cavity of the wall, thirsty and hungry. He lay in his room, feeling the metal bands that were now in his pocket. His first opportunity to retrieve the animal would be after dark.

In the afternoon, when Lydia had put down her stitching and was sitting in the courtyard with a friend, Amon announced that he was going to look for Marco.

"I'll be down at the yachting circuit," he said as he went out into the alleyway.

It was hot. Everyone was outside, making the most of their day off. Children were playing hopscotch in the dust and neighbours were talking across the walls of their courtyards.

When Amon reached the yachting circuit, the

place seemed deserted. There wasn't a breath of wind. If Marco was around, he'd be in the yacht house, working on his craft.

Amon had begun walking over to the building when he heard footsteps behind him.

"Looking for Marco?" asked Hester when she'd caught up with him.

Amon shoved his hands into his pockets. "Yeah."

"Me, too." She paused and looked out at the circuit, or perhaps beyond it to where the horizon shimmered in the sun. "So, no problems with this morning then?"

"It's okay."

"You *did* let it go?"

"I told you, it's okay."

"I was just curious, that's all."

"I'm curious, too," said Amon.

"Are you?"

"How did you know that it was the bird they were looking for? How did you know it had been seen?"

Hester drew in her breath and let it out in a long sigh. Then she turned her head to look at Amon, as if trying to decide something.

"How do I know I can trust you?" she asked.

"You don't," said Amon. "But the fact is, we both have secrets. Doesn't that somehow make us equal?"

She thought for a moment. "Maybe."

"So, are you going to tell me how you found out what the search was for?"

"Are you going to tell me what else it is that you know?"

He looked at her, trying to read her thoughts, trying to make up his mind if he should tell her about the bands.

"You're keeping something from me," she said. "Something you've learned about the bird."

He wriggled the toe of his shoe into the dust. It was so risky. How did he know he was safe with her? All he had to go on was that, so far, she hadn't told the Secure Division about the bird and — what was it that Marco had said about her? That she was a "good" person.

The metal bands from the bird's legs rattled in his pocket. Amon *did* trust Marco.

"Okay," he said at last. "We'll talk. But what we say goes no further."

"Agreed."

"You first," said Amon.

"Let's sit," she said. She settled herself down on the ground. Amon did the same.

"Well," she began, "let's just say that work with the Future Division isn't quite what I expected."

He waited.

"I went there expecting that I would be used in the areas where I had the greatest interest — and talent. Where I had the best chance of making discoveries and developing new — better — ways of living."

"And?"

"At the initial interview, I explained that I was very interested in researching water conservation, in developing a closed system where, basically, anything that lived, lived indoors."

"That's not a new idea."

"It's not, but the computer engineering systems involved in managing ventilation on that scale — ventilation that would prevent the spread of crop and human disease — are new."

"And?"

"No one wanted to know about it."

"So what *are* you working on?"

Hester laughed bitterly. "I'm exploring more

efficient ways of ripening tomatoes in the cool season." She paused. "At least, that's what I do during the day."

"Go on."

"Everyone has their own key to the labs. I've been going back for two or three hours at night to work on my own research."

"No one else is there?"

"No." She drew a circle in the dust with her finger. "It's just me and my computer. I have access to all the research that's been carried out over the last twenty years. It's all there, every bit of it, if you know where to look."

"And?"

"I began searching for any work in the past that had been done on the ventilation of closed systems. It didn't surprise me that I wasn't the first to have an interest in it. I found work by at least thirty employees of Future Thinkers. There's probably more there."

Amon waited for her to continue.

"The thing is, none of the research is complete. It all seems to just . . . fizzle out."

"Why don't you contact the researchers? Ask them why they stopped their work?"

Hester looked up at him. Her jaw was set in a firm line. "I'm not stupid, Amon. It's the first thing I did — at least, *tried* to do. The fact is, of the thirty researchers whose papers I've found, not one is still alive."

"They died. *All* of them?"

"They all contracted some form of serious illness. They didn't die naturally, Amon. They were retired."

"But, it's not possible. I mean . . ."

"How many more researchers into the same field would I need to dig out of the computer files, and then search for, before I came to the same conclusion?" she asked. "I don't need to look further, Amon. Those people, those scientists — their work wasn't wanted. Their research was terminated."

"So, aren't you afraid that . . ."

"Of course, but the difference is, I'm not recording anything on the subject on my computer because I'm not interested in closed systems and ventilation any more. What I want to know now is why they — our 'Leaders' — are so desperate to stop any research on the subject."

"You still haven't told me how you know the bird was sighted."

"Oh, that was a fluke. I told you that I found the alert on my screen when I went back to the lab last night?"

Amon nodded.

"Well, I happened to be walking past my Supervisor's office. It's a glass-walled office and it's locked at night, but his computer was still on and the screen was half facing towards me. I suppose he bumped it around, accidentally, when he was walking out of his office. Anyway, on the screen was the same alert that I then found on my own computer. But there was an addition to it. It said that an animal was in the community — a bird. It had been sighted at 9.45 pm by the border patrol."

"Border patrol?" asked Amon. "*What* border patrol? Ledron doesn't have a border patrol any more."

Hester looked again towards the horizon. "Exactly."

Amon followed her gaze.

"What's going on, Amon?" she asked. "How much about Ledron don't we know?"

Chapter Thirteen

When Hester had gone, Amon sat where he was, gazing out over the yachting circuit. Once, life had seemed so certain. It was hard, tedious even, but not frightening. As long as you lived by the rules and did not question anything, you were safe, and, whenever he wanted comfort or reassurance, there was Lydia to turn to. Now Amon's whole world was changing. It was no longer simply a case of obeying. Now he had to think for himself, and for Lydia, too — and the decisions he had to make were terrifying.

He felt in his pocket for the metal bands from the bird's legs. He had shown them to Hester. She had been wide-eyed, acknowledging, as he had, that they were an indication of life outside the community. Like Amon, she had been puzzled by the six numbers on the second tag.

"Freedom," she'd said, holding the third tag in her hand and letting the word roll across her tongue. "Do you think that someone — whoever engraved those numbers and letters on the tags — is trying to communicate with you?"

Amon had frowned. "You think the bird might actually be being used — deliberately — to bring messages?"

"It's possible."

Amon had wanted to tell her about Lydia's illness then, but he hadn't. He wasn't yet ready to trust her entirely.

"I've got to think about all of this," she'd said, standing up and brushing the dust from her jeans. "I was going to see Marco, but now I have to have some time to myself." She'd started to walk away, then looked back. "Tell Marco I'll see him tonight," she'd said.

In the yacht house, Marco was alone. He was sitting on the edge of a workbench, staring down at a shining yellow and blue sand yacht. Its body tapered to a long, sleek nose cone and on its sides were painted the numbers "one-six".

Amon whistled softy. "Where did *that* come from?"

Marco looked up at him. "It's mine," he said flatly.

"*Yours*? But it's brand new."

"I know."

"How did you . . . I mean who . . ."

"I've been given it."

Amon didn't understand.

"I'm being 'encouraged'," said Marco, "because they say I've got talent."

"*They*? It's from the top then? From the Leaders?"

"Yep. One of the Supervisors called at the hostel after dinner last night. She said I was to come down to the yacht house. When I got here, she showed me this."

"It's so awesome!"

Marco jumped off the workbench and wiped the sides of the yacht with the soft cloth he was holding.

"*Isn't* it?" asked Amon hesitantly.

"I guess," replied Marco. "It's just that it seems kind of weird that I've been given it."

Amon thought so, too, but he tried to make light

of it, for Marco's sake. "It's fantastic. Well done."

"I've seen a couple like it," said Marco, still sounding lost. "Not from our section of the community, though. A few months ago, some guys were racing them on the circuit for a couple of weeks. I didn't get a chance to talk to them and I haven't seen them since — or the yachts."

"Bet you can't wait for some wind to take it out. Two-seater, too. Guess that means I could come with you."

Marco hopped into the seat of the yacht and rested his feet on the pedals. Then he smiled and shook his head. "I'm crazy. I've been given this incredible new yacht and I'm sitting here worrying about it. You know what? I'm just going to enjoy it. Someone thinks I'm good enough for it — and I'm not going to argue with them. Bring on the wind!"

When Amon returned home in the afternoon, Lydia was lying on her bed, her stitching on the floor beside her.

"You okay?" he asked.

"I think my arm is swelling up again," she told him. "It's starting to feel tight."

Lydia held out her arm and he ran his fingers across the skin. It was no longer puffy, but taut and almost shiny.

"You should wear something with long sleeves," he said.

Lydia looked frightened. "Do you think so? Do you think people will notice?"

"Just wear a long-sleeved shirt to be on the safe side. You don't want anyone asking questions."

Lydia looked straight ahead. Amon could see the fear in her eyes. He reached out and held her hand. "Mum, I know you're scared. So am I. But there *is* a way out of this. I can't say what it is right now, but you have to trust that I know what I'm doing."

"You're all I have, Amon." She looked at him. Tears began to trickle down her cheeks. "You're almost a man," she said softly and squeezed his hand.

"I know," he told her, "and that's exactly why you have to trust me."

After dark that night, when the community lights had been turned out, Amon slipped from his room into the courtyard and knelt down beside the wall. Each tiny scraping as he removed the mortar from around the loose rock seemed so loud that he was sure he would be heard. He took out the stone, reached in for the box, then sealed up the hole once more.

Back in his room, he let out the bird. It was very much alive. It drank and drank from the water he had brought back from the dining room in his mouth. When he fed it on the mashed beans he had plastered to the inside of his sleeve, it gulped them down hungrily. Then it began to preen its feathers.

Amon lay back on his bed watching it, but his mind was elsewhere. It was time to begin planning seriously. The moment could no longer be put off. There was no way of knowing how long it would be before Lydia's condition was discovered. Amon ran over in his mind all that must be considered.

If he and Lydia left Ledron in search of another community, how long would the journey take? He tried to work out how far the bird could travel without water — a day, two days? With a strong wind and some careful sailing, could he travel just as fast as it — faster?

He and Lydia would need water for the journey. They could probably manage without food, but, without water, travel would be impossible. He searched in his mind for a source. There was no way he could smuggle water in that quantity from the dispenser, not with the guard watching all the time. The only water that might be unguarded was the trickle from the irrigation system in the greenhouses where Lydia worked. But the greenhouses were locked at night. He would have to think more about that later.

At least, thought Amon, he was no longer afraid of sailing a yacht over long distances. He was confident of his skills now, and Marco had said he was a natural. He had a feel for the wind and for the yacht he sailed. He was sure he would be just as comfortable in a two-seater — a yacht in which Lydia could ride with him.

What worried Amon more than anything, though — what made such a journey seem out of the question — was that he had no idea which direction he would sail in once they left Ledron.

And what of the border patrol? What was out there in the desert? The bird had been spotted, but by whom? And, if the bird had been spotted *entering* the community, then he and Lydia might equally well be observed *leaving* it.

Amon tugged off his jeans and wriggled into bed. There were so many questions to answer and time was running out. He looked down at the resting bird.

"Sleep well," he whispered to it. "Tomorrow morning, before it's light, you have to leave."

Chapter Thirteen

Chapter Fourteen

In the following week, Amon thought constantly about when he and Lydia should leave Ledron. The more he thought about it, the more terrifying the idea seemed. If only he could be sure that they would find the community that he was convinced was out there. More and more, his hope rested on the bird.

It had left him a week ago, flying with practised ease from his window ledge into the darkness of early morning. Each night, Amon left his window open, hoping that it might return with another message — one that would convince him that his plan to flee Ledron was the right one.

While he waited, he practised at the yachting circuit. Then, one afternoon, he broached the topic of a two-seater craft with Marco.

"Why do you want a two-seater?" Marco asked.

"I want something bigger, something faster. I reckon I'm over that little learner," he said, trying to keep his voice casual.

Marco laughed. "Suit yourself. It's not that different to sailing a single-seater, except when you've got someone else in it."

Amon listened closely.

"When you've got someone beside you, it's not just your own weight you have to think about when you're tacking," he explained. "If your passenger doesn't shift and lean like you do, you're going to flip the yacht, no matter how good you are."

"You mean, you have to train the passenger as well?"

"Exactly."

"Do you think you could show me how to sail with a passenger?" asked Amon hopefully.

Marco looked at his watch. "If you've got half an hour now, I could start you off, but then I have to go out for my own training."

Amon nodded. "Sure," he said. "I understand. The race is on Saturday, isn't it?"

"Yeah. Saturday at midday. Are you going to be there?"

"Of course," said Amon. "Isn't everyone going?

What's the competition looking like?"

Marco shrugged. "Hard to tell. The other sailors are good, but it's not until you get to race against them that you really see what someone can do."

"How are things going with Hester?" Amon asked as he and Marco signed out a two-seater for Amon and pushed it on to the track.

"Okay," said Marco with a smile, "but I reckon she's working way too hard. She's taking this research really seriously. It's more than just a job to her."

Amon watched as Marco rigged the yacht. Then they both donned helmets, climbed into their seats and strapped themselves in. Amon took the controls.

Out on the track, Marco shouted commands as Amon manoeuvred the craft. The yacht was heavier than the single-seater and felt sluggish and slow to respond. But, by the end of the half-hour, he was appreciating the steadiness of the machine and the increased speed as the wind filled a sail that was half the size again as that of his single-seater.

"It's all about learning to move together," said Marco when they were on their way back to the start of the track. "You and your passenger have to be a single body, but with you in charge."

Amon nodded. "I might take my mum out for a ride," he said. "She can give me the practice at having a passenger."

"Good idea," agreed Marco. "Can you take the yacht back when you're finished with it?"

"Sure," said Amon. "Thanks for the lesson."

When Marco had gone, Amon walked around the yacht, studying it carefully. Apart from a small space behind each of the seats, there was no storage capacity on board. For the journey, he and Lydia would need to carry water containers and extra clothing to wear at night, when the desert temperatures dropped by up to ten degrees. Lydia would be able to hold most of the gear on her lap. The rest would have to be strapped to the hull. Amon made a mental note to find some straps. They would use the sail to shelter under at night. They could wrap themselves in it and use the side of the yacht as protection against the wind.

Amon looked across to the sand-grey stone walls of Ledron's houses. His gaze took in the towering wind turbines that whirred and spun day and night, the vast enclosures of the greenhouses, the fields of wheat and cotton that stretched out to the north. This community was all he had ever known. It was his one source of life. Now he must leave it and sail into a waterless desert, because it could not promise him the one thing he wanted most: the chance of life for Lydia.

He swallowed hard. Worst of all, now that he knew of the bird, of the existence of life outside Ledron, and of the border patrol, he felt cheated and lied to. He felt like . . . He searched in his mind for the word. A prisoner, Amon decided. In Ledron, he felt exactly like a prisoner.

He turned back to the yacht. He had another hour of practice left and he was determined to master the new craft as swiftly as possible.

Amon didn't see Marco again before his race, at least not to speak to. Whenever he went to the circuit, Marco was out in his yacht, racing at high speed around the course, and at work they had been set different tasks. Despite that, he'd noticed that for a couple of days Marco hadn't even turned up.

"Will you be as good as him one day?" asked

Lydia as she sat nervously beside Amon in the two-seater.

"Doubt it," said Amon with a laugh.

Lydia had agreed to be Amon's passenger while he mastered the new yacht, although she had no idea what she was being prepared for. Amon was pleased with her. She seemed to trust him, to be willing to follow his commands quickly and exactly. He may not have been taking full advantage of the wind but they were able to sail steadily and reliably. There was never any chance that they would tip.

"I feel perfectly safe with you," Lydia said to him one afternoon. "I just relax and let you handle everything."

"Good," Amon told her. "That's what you have to do."

On the Saturday of the race, Lydia was working a weekend shift at the greenhouse. Amon set out for the circuit and met Hester on the way.

"Nervous?" he asked.

"Confident." Hester smiled back at him. She lowered her voice. "Had any more feathered visitors at night?"

Amon shook his head. "Nothing. How about

Chapter Fourteen

you? Have you got any more information?"

"No."

"Are you still working on the tomato project?"

"Actually," said Hester, "I'm not. The Supervisors at Future Thinkers seem to have realised I'm capable of more than that. I'm with a team hunting for new well sites. It's interesting. I'm using what I learned in my geology classes. It's a challenge."

At the racing circuit, a large crowd had gathered. Amon recognised several well-diggers from his Division. Some were standing with their families, others were talking with the girls who worked at the gardens.

"There he is," said Hester.

She pointed to the yacht house where the racers were pushing their machines towards the circuit. Marco was in front, his racer gleaming in the sun. He was wearing a white suit of thin material that flapped in the wind. Down the sides were bands of blue and yellow, to match the colour of the racing stripes and numbers on the sides of his yacht.

"Where did he get the gear from?" asked Amon.

"He was 'given' it," said Hester. "Marco's been given quite a lot of things lately."

"Like the yacht, you mean?" asked Amon.

"Not just the yacht," replied Hester. She looked around, as if checking on who might be watching or listening. "He's been on extra water rations in the lead-up to this race."

"Extra . . ."

"Shh!" warned Hester. "He's not supposed to have told anyone."

"But who's giving him all this stuff?"

"Don't you think it's more important to know why?" asked Hester.

There was no more time to talk after that. The beginning of the race was announced and the eight competing craft lined up at the start of the circuit. There were two other yachts like Marco's. Amon noticed that the sailors using them also had suits like Marco's — ones that matched the colours of their yachts.

"Look," whispered Hester, pointing to a make-shift stand that had been erected close to the finish line.

Amon followed her gaze to where a group of Leaders had gathered, their black cloaks moving in the wind. Their hoods were pulled up and their dark sunglasses gleamed.

"Do they usually come to races?" Amon asked.

"They only come to see the best," whispered Hester. "Why do you think that is?"

A speaker read out the competitors' names. A moment later, with the crack of a starting pistol, the yachts were away. For an instant, the spindly craft staggered like drunken creatures. Then, in a matter of seconds, their sails were full and they soared, winding their way back and forth across the track. The turn at the far end was almost out of sight, but Amon was sure that he caught a glimpse of blue and yellow leading on the far side of the track.

"It's Marco," shouted Hester beside him when the yachts came into clear view again. "He's in the lead!"

The crowd began calling out. Some of the spectators leapt into the air.

"They've got another three laps to go after this," shouted Amon over the noise.

"But he's so far ahead of the others!" Hester shouted back.

In front of the watching crowd, the yachts took their second turn before heading back up the straight. A collective groan of sympathy went up as the craft behind Marco's turned too quickly, careered towards the edge of the track and ran into the path of an oncoming yacht.

With only six craft now in the race, Marco was still in the lead. As the yachts made their second, then third lap, he was challenged by a sailor in an equally impressive machine. Heading down the straight for the last time before the home run, it seemed that Marco would be passed. The crowd went wild. Hester and Amon screamed at the top of their voices.

"Go, Marco!" shouted Amon.

"He's going to tip! I can't look!" screamed Hester.

"No, he's got the wheel back on the ground," Amon reassured her. "Here they come. He's still in the lead."

Marco's only rival, the sailor in the red and orange stripes, was less than a metre behind him.

"Push it, Marco!" screamed Amon. "You can do it!"

Hester covered her eyes. "I can't look. I can't!"

"Marco, Marco, Marco!" Amon joined in with the crowd's chant, then found himself cheering at the top of his voice.

Chapter Fourteen

"He's done it!" shouted Amon. "Marco's won!"

Hester punched the air. "*Yes!*"

"Hurry, let's go and find him," she called, pushing her way through the crowd.

Amon followed but, when they reached the edge of the circuit, Marco had vanished.

"There he is," said Hester, pointing to the dark group drawing to one side of the crowd. "He's with the Leaders, and so is that sailor who came second."

Amon watched as Marco and the second-place competitor were led away from the spectators. One of the Leaders had his arm around Marco's shoulders. The others followed closely.

"I thought he'd want to see me," said Hester.

Amon sensed the disappointment in her voice. "Where are they going?" he asked. "Where are they taking him? Isn't there some sort of prize-giving ceremony?"

Hester looked puzzled. "I don't know," she said quietly. "I don't know where they're taking him."

"Neither do I," said Amon. "But there's something I don't like about it. I don't like what's happening."

Chapter Fifteen

"We'll go and see him," announced Hester. "We'll give him time to get back to his hostel and then we'll go and talk to him."

The crowd had thinned out and they were sitting on the ground, propped up against two boulders.

"That's so weird," said Amon, "the way the Leaders just whipped him away. It was like . . ."

"Like they owned him?" asked Hester.

"Yeah, exactly like that."

"It's felt like he's been 'owned' for a while now," said Hester. "I go and see him and it's like he hasn't got any time for me. I don't mean he doesn't *want* to spend time with me. It's just that he feels he owes someone something for all this stuff he's been given: the yacht, the mechanic, the extra water. So he has to put in the time out on the circuit. Last week he even got off well-digging duties for two days so he could fit in some extra practice."

"So that's where he was," said Amon. "I thought he must be sick or something. Doesn't he wonder what all this attention is about?"

"I guess," said Hester. "But he says he doesn't want to think about it. He loves yachting so much, he doesn't question why it is that he's been given the extra time and encouragement."

"But *you* do," said Amon.

Hester looked into the distance. "I question everything now," she said. "And I know that, eventually, it's going to get me into trouble."

Amon waited for her to continue.

"I can't be sure," she said slowly, "but, at work, I think my computer use is being monitored."

"How can you tell?"

"It's just that, when I log on, I never speak in my password. I just say 'remember'. But this week, when I went to start up, that function wasn't an option. I had to speak in the password again."

"So?"

"It was as though someone had been working at the computer before me, someone who'd spoken in my password and then not reset the function to 'remember'. I mean, I could be mistaken. I might have changed the function myself without meaning to. But, somehow, I don't think so."

When Amon and Hester went to Marco's hostel an hour after the race, they weren't surprised to find he wasn't there. What did shock them was that all Marco's belongings had gone. His room was empty.

"What's going on?" Hester asked. Her voice was unsteady.

"Let's ask around," said Amon. "Someone must know something."

But most of the people in the hostel had been at the race and were puzzled as well.

"You should ask the Hostel Supervisor," said one of the residents. "I saw him in his office half an hour ago."

"We're looking for Marco Climmons," said Amon when they found the Supervisor. "He's in Room 12."

"At least, he *was*," added Hester. "All his things have been cleared out of his room."

"That's the yachting boy," said the Supervisor. To Amon he seemed to be less interested in the situation than he should be. Or was that just the impression he was trying to give them? "He's not with us now," he said.

"What do you mean?" asked Hester. "Where's he gone?"

The Supervisor looked casually at the screen in front of him. "Can't say for sure," he drawled laconically. "Someone came for his things this afternoon, round about one-ish."

"Just after the race finished," said Hester quietly. She turned to the Supervisor. "Don't bother yourself any more. We'll find him for ourselves."

Outside the hostel compound, Amon and Hester looked at each other blankly.

"Ledron has five and a half thousand people living in it," said Hester. "So where do we start looking?"

"You keep asking around at the hostel," said Amon. "Ask people as they come back in the evening. I'm going to the circuit. Someone down there might know something."

"We'll meet up later," said Hester. "I'll see you down at the racetrack before dinner."

At the circuit, Amon went straight to the yacht house. A couple of sailors were still working on their machines.

"Someone came for his yacht about an hour ago," said Ben, a sailor Amon had met before.

"Any idea where they were taking it?" he asked.

"They didn't say, but you could try the yacht house on the west side. It's right beside the canola oil processing plant. It's the only other place I know where they store yachts."

Amon didn't know the west side well, except that the Leaders' precinct was over there somewhere. He vaguely remembered a school visit to it when he was a kid. If he hurried, he'd make it there in half an hour.

It was strange wandering through a part of Ledron he wasn't familiar with. Though the houses all looked the same, there were unfamiliar faces and strange buildings. He passed a cotton-spinning plant and a water purification station that was well guarded by members of the Secure

Chapter Fifteen

Division. They watched him pass with bored expressions on their faces.

Then Amon was passing the high walls of the Leaders' precinct. The welcoming signs seemed strangely out of place outside the tall, locked and guarded gates.

He walked swiftly past, asked for directions to the yacht house from some kids playing ball in the street and was soon standing outside the building. He pushed open the door and was amazed to find Marco staring back at him.

"We've been looking for you," said Amon bluntly. "Hester and I went to your hostel, but you'd gone."

Marco didn't respond. Instead, he crouched down beside his yacht and began adjusting a bolt on the front wheel.

"Marco?"

"Sorry, Amon," he muttered, "but you shouldn't be here."

"Huh? I don't get it."

Marco kept working on the wheel, but Amon wasn't going anywhere. Not until he got some answers.

"Is that the trophy?" he asked, pointing at a

shield on the table behind Marco.

Marco stood up and passed it over to him.

"It's cool," said Amon.

Behind the boys, a door slid open. Marco glanced up nervously as a woman dressed in a Supervisor's uniform wandered over. She looked at Marco, but said nothing.

"You'd better go," said Marco to Amon.

"But what — I mean, are you living over here now, on the west side?"

Marco nodded.

"So, I'm not going to get to see you often?"

"I'm going to be pretty busy," said Marco.

"Busy doing what?"

The Supervisor coughed quietly.

"Can't say," said Marco. "It's probably best if . . . if you don't come looking for me again."

Amon felt hot and uncomfortable. He wanted to jump across the yacht and shake Marco, to make him sound and behave like the friend he knew.

"You *do* want to be here, don't you?" asked Amon.

Marco nodded. "Yeah, I do. I've been offered some big opportunities in yachting and I've decided to accept them."

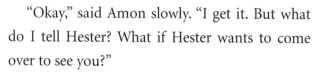

"Okay," said Amon slowly. "I get it. But what do I tell Hester? What if Hester wants to come over to see you?"

"I don't think she'll be doing that," said Marco in a knowing way.

For a moment, the boys looked at each other, neither of them saying anything. Then Amon turned towards the door.

"See you round then," he said. "If you change your mind and want some company, you can always . . ."

"See you round," said Marco.

Chapter Sixteen

Amon hurried back through the streets with an empty, sick feeling in his stomach. Marco had seemed like a different person — a stranger. It wasn't that he was behaving arrogantly because he had won the race. It was as though he now had something important to do, some opportunity that he valued above his friendship with Amon — and with Hester.

Amon turned the corner that led to his home, still wondering how he was going to tell Hester about the change in Marco, and there she was, sitting in the courtyard outside his room. She stood up when he walked in.

"What's wrong?" he asked, seeing the worry in her eyes.

"Amon, it's your mum."

"What's happened to her?"

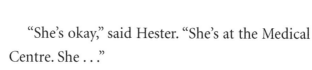

"She's okay," said Hester. "She's at the Medical Centre. She . . ."

"At the Medical Centre! Why is she there? Who took her? What happened?"

"Listen, Amon, I said she's okay. She's just injured her foot slightly. It's nothing serious."

"But how did it happen?"

"She dropped a crate of seedlings on it."

Amon's face was white.

"It could happen to anyone," Hester told him.

"I've got to find her."

"She'll be back any minute."

"No, you don't understand. I have to . . ."

"Here she is now," said Hester.

"It's just my foot," said Lydia, hobbling into the courtyard. "I've bruised it quite badly."

"But did they take tests?" asked Amon. "Did they test you for anything else?"

Hester looked from Amon to Lydia, puzzled.

"They did a general check-up," said Lydia. She pressed her lips together, hard. "They'll have the results in a week."

Amon stood completely still.

Lydia was on the verge of tears. "I'm going to lie down," she said.

"You go with her," said Hester.

"I will," replied Amon. "But first, tell me how you found out what had happened."

"I went looking for you at the circuit," Hester told him. "When I didn't find you, I came back here. Your neighbours told me what had happened. Amon, what is it about your mother that you're not telling me?"

Amon's eyes flicked towards the door of the house. Could he tell her? He so wanted to tell someone, to share the burden of his worry.

"Come into my room," he said.

When they were inside, Amon told Hester exactly what was wrong with Lydia, and what it was that he planned to do.

"But you can't just leave Ledron!" gasped Hester. "You don't even know which direction to sail in."

"I'll keep going until I find the way."

"And, if you ever reach another community, how do you know they'll take you in?"

"It's a risk I have to take."

"And the border patrol . . . ?"

"Whatever that is," said Amon. "Look, Hester, I didn't say it would be easy. I just said that I was going to do it. I don't have a choice."

"Did you see Marco?" she asked suddenly.

"Yes, I saw him."

"You don't have to tell me what's going on," said Hester. "I already know. I called in at the lab on my way to your place. I'd left some notes there that I needed to collect. When I turned on my screen, there was a message waiting for me from my Supervisor."

"What did it say?" asked Amon suspiciously.

"It said that the Future Division no longer thinks it suitable that I see Marco Climmons."

"What!" exclaimed Amon. "Did they give a reason?"

"None," said Hester. "They don't have to."

She looked down at her hands and began picking at the skin around her nails, making it bleed. "What's going on, Amon? Why have they taken Marco away? What do they want him for?"

When Hester had gone, Amon sat quietly on the edge of his bed. It was strange but, now that he had a time frame in which to work, now that he knew that he and Lydia must flee Ledron before the end of the week — before Lydia's test results were known — he felt strangely calm. It was as if he no longer needed to make decisions. They were being made for him.

He stood up. It was time to tell Lydia everything he knew.

"But it's not possible," she interrupted. "I mean, there can't be a bird. The Leaders have told us that . . ."

Amon continued with his explanation of the plan to flee.

"It's too dangerous," she said when he had finished. Her face was white, the fingers of her hands covered her cheeks. "I won't let you do it. It doesn't matter what happens to me. *You're* all that matters."

"Do you think I want to stay here, knowing what I know?" he asked. "We're living a lie. There *is* life outside this community. We may not know what it's like, but whoever sent that bird calls it 'freedom', and that's more than we have here."

Lydia studied her hands. "We'd leave by yacht?" she asked, her voice little more than a whisper.

"That's right," said Amon. "I'll stay behind at the yacht house one evening after practice. I'll say I'm working on the two-seater. Last one to leave the building pulls the door shut behind them — and that will be me. As soon as it's dark, we'll set sail. All you have to do is meet me down there."

"You make it sound so simple," said Lydia.

"You're a good passenger, Mum. You know how to balance, how to lean when we tack. Slowly and surely, we'll get there."

"Get *where*?" she asked, fear in her eyes. "Get *where*?"

When he didn't reply, she said, "You've been preparing me. That's why you've been taking me sailing, isn't it?"

"That's right." He moved to sit on the edge of her bed. "Mum, do you have any ideas about how we could find water to take with us? I thought you might know of some way we could get access to a supply through the greenhouse irrigation system."

Lydia was silent. After a time, she looked up.

"Joanie — you know her, she's the senior officer at work, the one I play chess with. She has a key to the pump room."

"Go on," said Amon.

"She uses it to get access to the pump every couple of hours. Then she has to return the key to the Supervisor's office at the end of the day. She's supposed to keep it with her at all times during work hours, but usually she leaves it in her bag . . . "

"It's too risky," said Amon. "If you were spotted . . . "

"Her bag — it's almost identical to my own. Sometimes I've actually picked it up by mistake. No one would notice if I took it to the bathroom with me. If I was found out, I'd only have to say it was a mistake."

"So, some time during the day, you would let yourself into the pump room and fill whatever containers you could find."

Lydia nodded. "The pump room isn't visible from the rest of the greenhouse. It's hidden behind a wall of tomato plants. There are always empty fertiliser concentrate bottles lying around. I could fill a couple at a time. I could do that for two or three days."

"You'd have to hide them somewhere."

"I'll choose extra-large overalls from the hanger

in the mornings. If I wear a belt underneath them, I can strap the containers on to it until I get a chance to load them into my own bag."

Amon nodded. "It's possible," he said. "I only wish you weren't the one who had to do it."

"Leave it to me," said Lydia. "After all, I've got nothing to lose, have I?"

Chapter Seventeen

On Wednesday evening, Lydia returned from work looking pale and drained, but her bag was heavy when Amon took it from her and he knew she had succeeded in getting the first load of water. They said nothing until they were inside. Then Lydia sank on to the bed.

"I was so frightened," she said. "Frightened I'd be seen going into the pump room. Frightened that someone would pick up my bag before I left work."

"But you did it," said Amon, taking her hand. "You did it, Mum, and you can do it again. There's nothing to stop us now."

"When will we go?" asked Lydia, her voice quiet.

"The wind is supposed to increase in strength on Friday," Amon told her. "I checked the forecast with one of the wind-generator engineers who sails. He knows what he's talking about."

"They might not want us," said Lydia suddenly.

"They?" asked Amon.

"Whoever we find out there," said Lydia. "Wherever we go, they might not take us in."

"It can't be worse than what's waiting for you here, can it?" said Amon bluntly.

Lydia fumbled in her pocket and drew out a note. "That girl, the one who was here on Saturday night? She found me at work today."

"Hester?"

"I think that's her name," said Lydia. "She asked me to give you this note."

Amon scanned the brief message. Hester wanted him to meet her at the library at six. It was almost that time now.

"I have to go out for a while," he told Lydia. He picked up her bag. "I'll keep this in my room. Tonight, after dark, I have a place where I can hide the water."

He left the water containers in his room and headed for the library. Hester was waiting for him, seated in front of a screen at the back of the room. There were several other people in the library and

Amon sat at a screen in the booth beside Hester's. They spoke in whispers. She wasted no time in telling Amon her news.

"The numbers," she said, in a voice that was excited but barely audible. "The numbers on the metal tag from the bird's leg. I think I know what they mean."

Amon's eyes widened.

"One of the people at the lab is working on new well sites. He was using a map. He was identifying possible digging sites using co-ordinates."

"I know all about co-ordinates," said Amon. "Those numbers, the ones from the bird's tag, they're *not* co-ordinates."

"Not co-ordinates that mean anything to *us*," said Hester, "which is why at first I didn't recognise them for what they are."

Amon looked puzzled.

"We've only ever worked with local maps," she said. "But if, for a moment, you start to believe that there *are* other habitable places besides our own community, then you begin to realise that there must be maps of those places, too, and that the co-ordinates on the bird's legs could relate to them."

Amon's mind began doing somersaults. All his life he had thought only locally, as if nothing existed outside of Ledron. Now it seemed that the world was a bigger place.

"I've done some calculations," said Hester. "I've extended the maps, if you like. If we treat the numbers from the tag as co-ordinates, then the position you're looking for is approximately four hundred and twenty kilometres away to the south-east."

Amon made some fast calculations in his head. "If we didn't meet any obstacles, and if the wind was steady, we could be there in less than fourteen hours."

Hester nodded.

"If there was some way for you to come with us . . ." Amon began, but Hester shook her head.

"I'm not leaving Marco," she said. "I have to find out what's going on. I don't trust whatever it is the Leaders have planned for him." She paused. "When will you leave?"

"Friday," Amon told her. "As soon as it's dark."

"Are you scared?" she asked bluntly.

"No more scared than I am staying here."

"I probably won't see you before you leave."

"No."

"I won't know if you . . ."

"If we make it?" asked Amon. "No, I guess you won't." He smiled bravely. "Thanks, Hester. Take care of Marco — if you can."

Hester smiled back. She leaned forward, as if she might hug him. Then she pulled back, stood up and walked swiftly out the door.

Amon switched on the screen and typed into the search box, "direction-finding using the sun".

On Thursday evening, when Amon arrived home from work, he found Lydia curled into a tight ball on her bed.

"I can't do it," she said. "I can't let *you* do it."

He sat beside her. "Did you get more water?"

She nodded.

"Be brave," he said.

"I want your father," said Lydia, her voice as soft as a little child's. "It's not fair that he went away like that, without telling me he was sick, without talking with me about the future."

"And if he was here," said Amon, "what would he want you to do?"

Lydia thought. Her body seemed to relax a little. She smiled weakly. "He would tell me to be brave," she said.

That night, Amon went to the yacht house. He checked that he was booked to use the two-seater for the last slot on Friday. Then he did a thorough check of the rigging.

The ropes were strong, the pulleys well-oiled. He propped the craft up and checked its undercarriage, tightening bolts and greasing and oiling the axles. He tried to remember all that Marco had taught him about maintaining the machine.

At last there was nothing more he could do. He waited until the last person had gone from the building and then began searching for something to strap luggage on to the hull of the yacht. In a cupboard at the back of the building, he found some straps. He pushed them to the back of the shelf. Then he took a sail-mending kit from a box and stowed it with the straps. He clicked off the light switch and went out of the yacht house, closing the door behind him.

It was pitch black outside. The sky was bright with stars. Amon stared out into the desert. In a short space of time he had adjusted to believing that there was life outside Ledron. He had learned to sail in order to find it. Now it was really going to happen. He was going to sail away from all the security he had ever known, into a world where his only hope was pinned on a message from a bird he had been told could not exist. He shook his head as if to clear his mind. He felt he was living in a dream.

Chapter Seventeen

Chapter Eighteen

At seven o'clock on Friday evening, Amon packed into a small bag the handful of his belongings he could carry on the yacht: the pocketknife that had belonged to his father, the emergency flashlight from his drawer, a thermal top and the windproof jacket he wore on well-digs. Last of all, he put into his pocket the metal tags he had taken from the bird's legs. There was still room for the few things he would collect from the yacht house.

The community meal was over and there was still an hour of light left. Amon went out of his room and closed the door behind him.

Lydia was in the house. He found her standing in the middle of the room. She seemed paralysed, unable to move in any direction.

"I've got a medical appointment tomorrow morning," she said, with panic in her voice.

"You won't be here for it," replied Amon calmly.

"I could be," she said. "We could forget all this. We could stay and . . ."

"No," said Amon firmly. "We're not doing that." He looked at her bag lying on the bed. "Have you packed everything you're taking?"

"Everything we have room for," she said.

"In a minute, I'm going down to the yacht house." He paused. "You're sure you know exactly how to get the water?"

She nodded. "As soon as the lights go out, I go to the wall and take out the stone. The four water containers are inside. I strap them on to the belt under my jacket."

"Good," said Amon. "And if anyone asks where you're going?"

"I tell them that my foot's hurting and that I'm going to the Night Medical Centre."

"Perfect," said Amon. "No one will question that. You have to go past the yacht house to reach it."

Lydia ran her tongue around her lips. "What time does the Secure Division check the yacht house?"

"Thirty minutes after the lights go out," Amon

told her. "So it works like this: at ten o'clock, off go the lights. You collect the water, strap it on and head for the yacht house. It'll take you five minutes to get the water and ten minutes to get to the yacht house. That gives us fifteen minutes to leave before the Secure Division arrives."

"Are you sure it wouldn't be better to collect the water earlier?"

"Absolutely not. It has to be done after dark or I'd take it myself. You can't run the risk of being seen."

He reached out for Lydia's arm and held it tightly. "There's a good wind blowing. Be brave," he said.

At the circuit, Amon pushed the two-seater on to the track. The wind whipped at the sail, making it crack hard until he pulled in the mainsheet. Then he was away, running with the wind, towards the orange glow of the setting sun. This was how he would sail after dark. For a start, he would let the yacht run. That way he would be free to concentrate on covering distance without having to think about direction. There would be time for that later. But, before anything else, as quickly as possible, they must get as far away from Ledron as they could.

He tacked back to the start of the track and pulled the craft up beside the yacht house. There were three other sailors working in the building. Amon recognised one of them as Daman, a digger from Marco's hostel.

"I saw Marco today," he called to Amon.

"Yeah. He's living on the west side now."

"He was coming out of the Leaders' Precinct," said Daman. "He's doing some kind of training over there."

"Did he say what it was?" asked Amon.

Daman shook his head. "He didn't say anything — didn't even want to know me. He's too good for us since he won that race. We're not worth speaking to."

"Weird," muttered Amon.

Daman wandered back to his yacht and Amon pretended to be busy on his own.

Just before ten, the other sailors all left the building together.

"Last one out locks the door behind them," Daman called back.

"I know," Amon told him. He hoped his voice sounded stronger than he felt.

As soon as they had gone, Amon reached for the few things he had stowed at the back of the shelf and stuffed them into his bag. He would fasten them, along with the water — when Lydia arrived with it — to the rear of the hull.

It was five minutes to ten. He reached for his flashlight and tightened its elastic bands over his head. In the last few minutes of light, he checked and rechecked the craft: wheels, mast, sails, ropes, pulleys, steering.

His heart was racing and he took a few deep breaths to calm himself. What worried him most was what he would find at the border. But there was nothing he could do about that now and, he reassured himself, there was no need to think of everything at once. First things first. Get Lydia into the yacht. Set sail and move as fast as he could away from Ledron.

Without warning, the lights in the yacht house flicked off. Amon switched on his flashlight and sprang into action. He wheeled the yacht to the front of the building. Then he checked outside for anyone who might be about. The coast was clear.

The wind was brisk. He rigged the yacht.

He looked at his watch. In just five minutes, Lydia would arrive. He tried to keep calm and not worry about her short walk with the water strapped to her sides. If she was stopped, she had her story. As long as she didn't panic, she would be all right — unless someone from the Secure Division decided to accompany her to the Night Medical Centre. Amon hadn't thought of that. His heart began racing again. Sweat gathered on his brow. He switched off his flashlight and went to the door to look for her. Where was she? If she was late . . . but he couldn't afford to think about that.

Then, out in the darkness, he saw her, a grey figure weaving towards him. A moment later, she was inside the building, shaking as she unbuckled the water bottles from around her waist.

"Did anyone stop you?" he asked, gathering the containers into a bag.

Lydia shook her head. "I . . . I have to sit down for a minute."

"Sit in the yacht, Mum," replied Amon. "I'll just strap this stuff on. Then I'll wheel everything down to the track."

"I can help."

"No, just sit, and hold on to your bag."

Amon drew back the big double doors of the yacht house, wincing at the grating noise of the rollers as they slid along their track.

"Right," he whispered to Lydia, "out we go."

The nose of the yacht inched forwards. Amon checked right and left. No one. He pushed the yacht out a fraction further.

"Amon!"

A voice hissed at him through the darkness. He spun round, poised to run. Lydia was half out of the yacht, the belongings on her knees scattering across the ground.

"Amon! Stop! It's me!"

Hester came running towards them.

"We've got to go — now!" Amon told her. "The Secure Division will be here in a few minutes."

"Listen to me, Amon. I'm begging you to do exactly what I ask. You're in danger. We all are. We can leave tonight, but . . ."

"*We?*"

"Yes, Marco will be here in a few minutes."

"But . . ."

"No buts, Amon."

"Listen to her!" said Lydia. "Do what she says."

"All right, all right!" agreed Amon. "What do we do?"

"Get the yacht back into the building," said Hester. She was already beginning to push it. "Then shut the doors. We'll have to hide in here while the Secure Division check the lock-up."

"Where?" wailed Lydia. "Where do we hide?" She shone her flashlight around the inside of the dark building.

"Under the yachts against the back wall," hissed Amon. "But first, I have to get this rigging down."

His fingers felt numb as he untied knots and lowered the sail on the two-seater. There was no time to take the water off the hull. He threw the sail over it instead.

Hester and Lydia were already flattening themselves against the floor under the yachts when Amon joined them. He wedged himself under a hull and breathed shallowly. Hester's face was just a few centimetres from his own.

The door to the building rattled open. They heard the voices of the Secure Division officers as they entered. The beams from their high-powered flashlights played over the walls and swept across

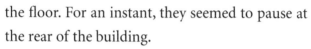

the floor. For an instant, they seemed to pause at the rear of the building.

"All set?" called one woman to the other.

"Looks fine," came the reply. "Let's lock."

The door closed with a bang and the key grated in the lock.

"Don't move yet," whispered Hester. "They might come back for something."

They lay against the cold floor for what seemed an eternity. Then Hester began wriggling out. "No one uses their flashlight," she said.

"Are you going to tell us what's going on?" demanded Amon angrily. "We could have been discovered just then. What's this about Marco?"

"Look," said Hester, "you have to trust me. I've been in touch with him. I'm expecting him to show up here any minute. At least, I hope that's what he'll do."

"He knows we're *leaving*?" exploded Amon. "You *told* him!"

"No. He knows *I'm* leaving," she said quietly. "And he knows that he's in danger. I hope that's enough to bring him here."

"We can't wait for him," insisted Amon.

"We can't go without him. We'll need him."

"What is she talking about?" asked Lydia. She turned to Hester. "What do you know that we don't?"

Chapter Eighteen

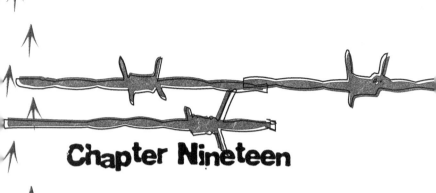

Chapter Nineteen

"I told you that I'd received a message from my Supervisor saying that I wasn't to see Marco again," began Hester.

Amon nodded.

"I must have seemed pretty upset because there was a woman at work who noticed and asked me about it. I told her about Marco winning the race and being taken away. Then, yesterday, she decided to tell me her own story."

"Which was what?" asked Lydia.

"She said the same thing happened to her five years ago. Only it was worse. She and her boyfriend were engaged. They were about to get married, but their wedding had to be postponed until after his first big yachting race — he was a brilliant sailor. Just like Marco, he was an orphan. And, just like Marco, he was given a lot of stuff by the Leaders — water, clothing, time off work, a new yacht."

"And then what?" asked Amon.

"He won the race," said Hester.

"And he was taken away and she wasn't allowed to see him again?" he guessed.

"Exactly," said Hester. "She was heartbroken, but there was nothing she could do. She tried to talk to him, but he told her they were finished. Then she didn't see him again — ever."

"What happens to these 'winners'?" asked Lydia.

"I'm not totally sure," said Hester, "but I have my suspicions. There are a couple of things I do know for certain. Every winner who has ever been taken away after winning a big race has been an orphan." She paused. "And their average life expectancy after being removed from the general community is three years."

Amon gasped. "So Marco's . . ."

"He's in danger," said Hester. "And so am I. I used my work computer to research the details of who had won major races and to try to track those people down. That's when I found out about their status as orphans and their life expectancy."

"You thought your computer activity was being monitored," he said.

"I did. In fact, I'm sure of it. So you see, Amon, there's no going back for me now. I have to leave. I'm a refugee, too."

"And Marco?"

"I had a letter delivered to him by a mutual friend. It outlined what I know. The rest is up to him."

"So he may turn up here tonight or he may not?"

A tap on the door sent them into silence.

"The Secure Division!" hissed Lydia. She was already diving for cover behind the yachts.

The tap came again.

"Marco?" whispered Amon.

"Let me go," said Hester. "He doesn't know you're here. If he can't be persuaded to come with us, I won't tell him anything about your plan. You'll still be safe to leave as soon as he's gone."

"But what if he turns you in? What if he has brought someone from the Secure Division with him?"

"I have to take that chance," said Hester. "I love him, Amon. I have to try to make him leave with me."

Lydia and Amon crept under the yachts again as Hester tiptoed across the wide floor. They heard the door open, then close. There was a murmur of muffled voices. Amon was almost certain Marco had arrived alone.

Lying under the yachts, it seemed to Amon that Hester and Marco would never finish talking, but then he heard the soft clicking of their shoes as they walked towards them. Lydia squeezed his hand tightly.

"You can come out," Hester said softly. "He's coming with us."

When Amon stood up, Marco stepped forward and hugged him tightly.

"Didn't think I'd see you again," said Amon roughly.

"Pretty strange place to meet," replied Marco.

"I've told him everything," said Hester. "I had to. We all hold pieces to this jigsaw puzzle we're in. By sharing them, we can start to see the whole picture."

"She's told me about the bird," said Marco. "And about the possibility of a border patrol. It all makes sense."

"What border patrol?" demanded Lydia. She

looked at Amon. "You didn't tell me anything about a border patrol."

"I don't know enough about it to tell you anything," said Amon.

"I think *I* know," said Marco. "At least, from what Hester's told me, I know enough to guess." He paused. "Since I won the race, I've been receiving military instruction."

"You've been taught how to *fight*?" Amon couldn't believe what he was hearing.

"That's right," said Marco. "I've been training in a simulator, learning how to capture a moving yacht."

"After hearing what I've told him," said Hester, "Marco believes he may be being trained as a border patrol guard. We think that orphans are chosen for training because no one will question their disappearance once they're sent on duty."

"But we're going out there," said Lydia. "We have to cross the border. What if we're caught?"

"We need to think carefully," said Marco. "But there's a limit to what we can plan for when we know so little."

"Well, we can assume *some* things," said Hester. Amon could see her analytical mind at work. "We know we've been lied to by the Leaders. There is life outside Ledron. The bird has proven that. We also know that it was spotted by the border patrol and an alert sent out. So, whoever or whatever is out there, it doesn't want anything to get in to the community."

"But what we don't know," said Marco, "is the strength of security out there. It's not as if there's an army being trained inside the Leaders' Precinct. There was only one other sailor training with me."

"They want people who can sail at speed," said Hester. "My guess is that there'll be yachts that patrol out there rather than a complete blockade. It would take too many people to maintain."

"There could be some sort of security fence," suggested Lydia.

"That's right," agreed Hester. "Which is why a bird made it into Ledron. It would be almost impossible to prevent anything flying over whatever border is out there."

"Birds — the simplest and most efficient threat to the security of Ledron," mused Amon.

"We can't stand around all night talking about this," said Marco. "If we're going to leave, and Hester, at least, has no choice but to go tonight, then we'd better do it."

"How do you want to organise things?" asked Amon.

"You stick to your plans to take Lydia in the two-seater," said Marco. "Hester and I will take another one. We'll sail together, fast at first, until we're out of sight of the community. Then we'll have to travel more slowly. We have to be on a constant lookout for anything that's out there."

"We have to see them before they see us," said Amon.

"Check outside," said Marco to Hester. "Once you give us the all-clear, we roll back the doors and wheel out the yachts. Then we go, straight out into the night, as fast as we can."

"I'll close the doors after us," said Hester. "If the Secure Division comes by and sees them open, they'll know something is wrong. And we want all the headstart we can get."

Chapter Twenty

As soon as the yachts were rigged, Hester opened the side door and stepped cautiously outside.

"All clear," she whispered back. "Go!"

The big doors ground open. Sitting in the seat of the yacht, Lydia held on fiercely to her bag. Amon and Marco pushed the machines across the dry ground and brought them to a halt at the edge of the track. The sails caught the wind and flapped.

"Get started," Marco instructed Amon. "We'll catch you up."

Amon slid into the seat beside Lydia.

"Hold tight," he warned. He pulled on the mainsheet and immediately the yacht rolled forwards. It gathered speed quickly, eating the wind and surging through the darkness like something alive. Amon felt the cool air rush against his face, drying the beads of sweat that had gathered on his brow.

"I can see them now," said Lydia, looking back. "They're on their way."

Amon pulled in more sail. They were almost at the far end of the circuit. This is it, he thought, as they left the track. There's no turning back now.

When Marco's yacht had caught up with theirs, Amon risked a quick look behind. Ledron lay in darkness, the tall towers of the wind turbines reflecting the light of a new moon. There was no way of knowing if they'd been seen, but he guessed not. For a moment, a wave of sadness washed over him. He was leaving a place he had known all his life, a place he could no longer call home.

They ran with the wind for fifteen minutes. Then Marco signalled for them to slow and Amon let out the mainsheet until the two craft were sailing parallel to each other.

"Let's take it slowly now," Marco called out. "Everyone's to keep a watch for what's ahead. The moment something's spotted, even if you only *think* you see something, we stop."

Amon was unused to sailing outside the circuit. The ground was uneven. Dips and hollows caught the wheels of the yacht and sent them bouncing up from their seats. Rubble and small rocks made it difficult to keep the craft on course. There was more steering involved than he had expected.

"Not so fast," begged Lydia as they bounced over another hummock.

Ahead of them, Marco's yacht slowed and came to a halt.

"What is it?" asked Amon, catching up.

"Turn back!" warned Marco. "Hester thinks she's seen something."

The yachts doubled back, weaving in the wind as they tacked.

"I can't be sure," said Hester a few minutes later, as the craft drew close together once more, "but I thought I caught a glimpse of something shining in the moonlight. Maybe it was a post. I don't know. It may have been nothing."

"I want you all to stay here," said Marco. "I'll sail back to where we were. Then I'll take down the rigging, so the yacht's less likely to be spotted, and continue on foot."

"I'm coming with you," said Amon.

Marco looked at him, as if considering the best thing to do.

"I am," insisted Amon.

"Get in then," said Marco as Hester slid out of her seat. "Lydia, Hester, don't move from this spot. We don't want to lose you."

It felt good to be sailing with Marco again. In spite of his own fear, Amon noticed the effortless way in which Marco handled the yacht. His work with the ropes and his balance and steering were seamless. It was as though he was a part of the craft itself.

"This is about as far as we came last time," said Marco.

The yacht turned sharply and came to a stop. Amon began taking down the sail.

"Ready?" Marco asked when they had stuffed it under the yacht.

Amon nodded.

Silently, they moved slowly forwards. The chill wind made Amon shiver. They had walked for five minutes before Marco stopped and motioned to Amon to lie down on the ground.

"I see them, too," whispered Amon.

"They're towers of some sort," hissed Marco. He stared into the distance. "They just go on and on in both directions."

"This is it," said Amon. "This is the border."

Marco nodded. "We'll have to go a bit closer to check it out. Ready to move?"

"Ready."

"Keep low," warned Marco.

They scrambled over the ground on their knees and elbows. Then Amon spotted something moving in the distance.

"Down!" he whispered urgently. They flattened themselves against the cold sand.

"I see it," whispered Marco. "It's a yacht."

"It's turning. It's going back the way it came."

"It's not on its own," hissed Amon. "Look, there's another coming from the opposite direction."

The second yacht reached a tower, turned and sailed back again.

"We'll wait," whispered Marco. "I want to see if they return."

A few minutes later, both yachts reappeared, turned, then sailed out of sight again.

"They're keeping some sort of regular watch," said Amon.

"Patrolling," agreed Marco. "They're big, too. Racers. There'll be two men on board each."

"Well-trained men," said Amon. "What do you

make of the towers?"

"I'm just guessing," said Marco, "but I'd say there's some sort of electronic fence operating between them. Crossing it probably sets off an alarm."

"And the patrol yachts respond," finished Amon.

"Let's get back to the others," said Marco. "We know enough for now."

"So," said Hester when Marco and Amon had returned, "it will be a matter of outrunning whoever's out there on the yachts. Is that what you're saying?"

Marco looked at her. "I think that's what it comes down to."

"But how can we?" asked Lydia. "If they really do choose the top sailors for the border patrol, how can we compete against them?"

"Marco's a top sailor, too," Amon reminded her.

Marco looked into the distance. "But I'm not sailing in a racer, like they are," he said. "Look, this is what I think: if Hester and Lydia take one yacht . . ."

"Me! Sail a yacht on my own?" Hester looked terrified.

"You're sailing well," said Marco. "You can do it."

"But not out here, not with the patrol yachts waiting for us. Why can't Amon sail with Lydia?"

"You and Lydia will cross first," continued Marco. "Amon and I will be right behind you. If you're spotted, keep going. We'll lag behind to act as a decoy. You and Lydia can get away."

"It won't work!" Lydia cried. "You'll never outrun them."

"We can," insisted Marco. "Amon's an excellent sailor and, with the two of us working together, plus a headstart, we've got a good chance."

"They're in racers," Lydia reminded them. "Can you outrun racers?"

Marco took a deep breath.

"It's the only way," interrupted Amon. "We can't go back and, unless we cross the border, we can't go forwards."

"What you're saying," said Hester grimly, "is that we're trapped. Unless we make a move, we're stuck here in no-man's land."

They stood together in the cold night. They had run out of choices.

Chapter Twenty

Chapter Twenty-one

It was Marco who took charge, gently guiding Hester toward Amon's yacht and reaching for the belt to buckle her in. When Lydia was settled into the seat beside her, Marco and Amon strapped themselves into their own yacht.

"Ready?" asked Marco.

Hester nodded and pulled in the mainsheet.

"Tighter," coaxed Marco. "And, remember, keep the wind over your right shoulder. That way, you'll sail as fast as possible. Stay on that course. Don't alter it, and we'll be able to find you."

Hester pulled on the rope again and, together, the two yachts sailed forwards until they reached the place where she had first spotted the towers.

"Sails down," ordered Marco.

They lowered the sails and began pushing the yachts. The sand squeaked beneath the wheels.

"Down!" warned Amon suddenly. "Patrol yacht to the right. It's passing the tower."

"Look left! Here comes the second one," said Hester.

Lying on the ground, Marco consulted his watch. "Is everyone sure what they're to do?"

The others nodded.

The patrol yachts had reached their respective towers and were turning and heading back in the direction they had come from.

"This is it," called Marco. "Go!"

They sprang to their feet. Hester winched up the sail of her yacht and Marco did the same to his own.

"Hurry!" pleaded Lydia.

They were in their seats and sailing towards the towers before there was time to reply.

Amon looked across at Lydia, sitting bolt upright, her eyes trained on the invisible line of the border. Hester's concentration was fierce as she gripped the mainsheet.

The towers were closer now, tall metallic posts standing thirty metres apart. They seemed to grow from the desert around them.

"This is your break," said Marco. He let out

the sail of his yacht a fraction, and Hester's craft sprang ahead of Marco's.

"Go for it!" he called.

Amon held his breath, but whatever it was that he was expecting — a siren, an electric field — nothing prepared him for what happened next.

"No!" Marco cried out as the desert burst into light.

Amon shielded his eyes against the intense brightness that swept down from the dazzling white lights on top of the towers. Blinded by the glare, Marco's steering faltered and the yacht swerved, dangerously close to tipping. Amon leaned hard to the port side to compensate. The starboard wheel thumped down as it returned to the ground.

Ahead of them, Hester was still in control, but it was as though she were sailing in a pool of daylight. And then Amon saw it, the first patrol craft bearing down on them, gleaming like a beacon as it entered the ring of light.

"Yacht to starboard!" he shouted to Marco. "It's heading in Hester's direction."

Amon wasn't sure what it was that Marco did next, but it was as though their own yacht received an extra boost of power from some unknown source.

"Got to get the patrol's attention," said Marco. "Got to get them interested in *us*."

Over the sound of the wind, a shout rang out.

"They've seen Hester," called Amon.

"She's still sailing," Marco shouted back.

Another shout echoed into the night.

"Yacht to port!" called Amon. "It's heading straight for *us*!"

The patrol yacht veered towards them. Marco's hand was white where the mainsheet stretched tight across his skin. They were well in the lead. If only they could maintain their speed, reach the ring of darkness and escape from the bowl of light that had them trapped.

As the yacht swung around to avoid the patrol yacht, a rock flew up and ricocheted off the metal of the mast. Amon ducked – but beside him, Marco had been flung back in his seat, wounded.

"Grab the mainsheet!" groaned Marco. "I can keep steering."

Amon struggled to grip the rope as Marco reached for his injured shoulder. A dark patch of blood was seeping steadily into the fabric of his shirt.

The patrol yacht closed in. Any minute now and they'd be caught.

Lying across Marco's legs, Amon pulled hard on the mainsheet. Marco, grimacing with pain, tried desperately to concentrate on his steering.

"Got to get more speed," he urged Amon. "Got to."

Amon saw what happened next as if in slow motion — one minute thinking they might be caught and, the next, realising that escape might be within their grasp. Looking in the direction of the patrol yacht, he could see it was gaining on them, faster and faster. Then, the front of the enemy yacht seemed to leave the ground and one guard toppled back, as he was jolted from his seat.

"They've hit rocks!" shouted Amon. "Man overboard. Keep steering, Marco. We're leaving them behind!"

The patrol yacht spun round to go back for the fallen guard. Hester and Lydia were out of sight ahead of them and the yacht that had been in pursuit of them was tacking back towards him and Marco.

"What's happened to Hester?" Marco asked, his voice strained with pain.

There was no time to reply before they heard a shout from the approaching yacht.

"Just about there," Amon said through clenched teeth. "Got to reach the darkness."

But a quick glance behind him confirmed Amon's worst fears. The first yacht collected the fallen sailor and was turned in their direction. There was no time for clever planning. The only thing that could save them now was sheer speed, and there was only one way to achieve that.

"Listen, Marco," said Amon, "don't ask any questions, just do exactly what I say. Steer us sixty degrees to starboard. Now!"

"I can't ... can't make my legs work ..." groaned Marco.

"Just do it!" Amon was almost screaming. "We've got to keep up our speed. I'm keeping the mainsheet tight as we go round."

"We'll capsize!"

"Not if we balance to my side! Now do it!"

Suddenly, Marco responded and the yacht spun round to run parallel to the border towers, increasing speed rapidly.

Amon leaned far out to the edge of the yacht. The ground beneath him seemed dangerously close as he sped over it.

"Get over here!" he called to Marco. "Get over or we're going to tip."

Marco struggled to shift his weight and Amon saw the strain in his face.

The patrol yachts were now both in pursuit, but the extra speed Amon had gained by the jibe had put them well in the lead.

"Get back in your seat!" Amon commanded when they had regained balance. "The patrols are gaining on us. When I give the word, we jibe again and run out towards the desert."

"Ready?" groaned Marco.

"Take it away," commanded Amon.

The yacht changed direction and, a moment later, with the wind directly behind them, their increase in speed was dramatic.

Perhaps sensing that they were losing the chase, the patrol yachts dropped back. Amon risked a quick look behind him, not daring to hope that they could be out of danger. But they were speeding away from the patrol yachts. Seconds later, at the edge of the brightness, darkness enveloped them like a soft black cover.

There was no way of knowing where they were heading now. They simply sailed with the wind behind them, putting as much distance as they could between themselves and the patrol yachts.

"I can't keep going for much longer," Marco moaned.

Amon glanced behind them. The light was a dim glow in the distance. And, strangely, the patrol yachts were nowhere to be seen.

"They've given up the chase," he said. "I don't know why or how, but it looks as if they're not interested in us any more."

"Got to stop," begged Marco again.

"Soon," Amon reassured him. "Soon we can stop."

The terrain was rockier now and the occasional large boulder loomed out of the darkness.

"Let the sail out," ordered Marco when they'd been travelling for about an hour. His voice was weak. "I can't carry on."

The rope slid through Amon's hand and the yacht slowed, then stopped.

"Can you get across here?" asked Amon, half dragging Marco into the passenger's seat.

Chapter Twenty-one

"It hurts," winced Marco. "I need water."

"You'll have water — as soon as we find the others." Amon looked into the darkness. *If* we find them, he thought. There was no way of knowing if they had outrun the patrol yacht or been . . . but he couldn't face the alternative.

In the darkness, it seemed an impossible task that they could find each other. But they had asked Lydia and Hester not to change direction. Surely, somewhere out here in the vast desert, they would be waiting for them.

Marco leaned back in his seat. His eyes were closed and his hand had fallen from his shoulder. Amon saw the tear in his shirt and the blood still seeping from the jagged wound. He reached down and tore a strip of fabric from the leg of his pants. He bound it as tightly as he could around the wound.

"Thanks," muttered Marco.

Amon buckled him in. Then he took control of the yacht and nosed it further out into the desert.

Chapter Twenty-two

It wasn't until dawn that the two yachts were reunited. Exhausted, Amon had stopped just before 1 a.m., worried about not having caught up with Hester and Lydia, but unable to carry on. Feeling the intense cold of the desert, he'd hauled down the sail and used it to cover himself and Marco. Then he'd fallen into a fitful sleep.

It was Hester's shouting that woke him. Like something out of a dream, she was sailing towards them, the yacht a pale shadow in the dim light, tacking methodically across the sand. Lydia was beside her, waving.

Amon leapt out of his seat and waved back.

"It's Hester! They've found us!" he told Marco.

Marco's eyes were closed, but he was awake. He responded with a weak smile as Amon ran to meet the others.

"We thought we'd never find you," called Lydia. She leapt from her seat and hugged Amon tight. "We thought you'd been captured, that the guards had . . ." Her voice broke and her shoulders rocked as she sobbed.

"We waited and waited for you," Hester told Amon. "Then, when it started to grow light, we retraced our own tracks back until Lydia spotted you in the distance."

"You did well to find us," he said.

"I don't understand why the patrol yachts just gave up chasing us," she said. "It was as though, as soon as we reached the darkness, they weren't interested in us any more."

"The same happened with us," said Amon, puzzled. "Once we were well over the border, they didn't want us any more."

Hester looked past him. "What's wrong with Marco?" she asked. "He's not moving."

"He's wounded," said Amon. "We hit some rocks. One hit him in the shoulder."

Hester's face drained of colour.

"You've still got the water?" asked Amon.

"We've only taken a few sips," Lydia told him.

"Good. Marco's been asking for water all night. And we'll need it to clean his shoulder."

Hester unstrapped a water container and ran towards Marco. She unscrewed the lid and let the liquid trickle slowly into his open mouth.

"Ohh — that's good," muttered Marco, his eyes fluttering open.

Lydia peeled back the bloodied fabric from his shoulder. Then she ripped a strip from the bottom of her shirt and used it to sponge the dried blood from the wound.

Marco winced. "I'm so hot," he said.

"I can see bone," said Lydia grimly.

Hester felt his brow. "He's burning up."

"His high temperature probably means that the wound is infected," said Lydia quietly, after they had moved a short distance away from Marco.

"There's nothing we can do about that," said Hester. "We've got no medication."

"What are you doing?" Lydia asked. She was watching Amon studying the sky, her eyebrows raised in astonishment.

"Taking directions," he replied. "We have to continue with the plan. We have to find help for Marco as quickly as possible." He turned to

Hester. "Do you think you can keep sailing? I've had some sleep, but you've had no rest at all."

Hester looked over at Marco. "I can keep going," she said.

Cleaning Marco's wound had depleted their precious water supply, but they each took a careful sip from what was left. Then, with Amon leading the way, they set sail.

As morning drew on, the heat of the day closed in. The sand shimmered in front of them. Now and again, they stopped to stretch their cramped legs and take their direction from the sun. Towards midday, Hester changed yachts with Amon so that she could be with Marco — though he was capable of making little response.

"Hungry?" she asked Amon as they made the swap.

He nodded.

"Scared?" he asked her.

"That we're lost? Sure, I'm scared."

"We brought enough water for two. We're sharing it among four of us," he said.

"You thought we might find the community by early evening."

"Let's get going then," he said.

At three in the afternoon, Hester brought her yacht parallel with Amon's.

"It's Marco," she called. "He's very restless. He keeps moving about. I think we need to stop, let him lie down and get some proper rest."

Amon looked anxious. "All right," he agreed. "Just for half an hour. I'll pitch a sail."

When they were out of the yachts and Marco was lying on the ground with Hester's jacket for a pillow, Amon arranged the sail to provide shade for them all.

Marco tossed and turned. Hester offered him a little water and, at last, he seemed to sleep.

Lydia slept, too, her head resting against her swollen arm.

"What a mess," said Amon. Perhaps he sounded as wretched as he felt, because Hester reached out to touch his arm. He looked out at the desert. "This just goes on and on."

"There *is* another community out here and we're going to find it," she said firmly.

"But when?" asked Amon. "We haven't got enough water left to see us through the night. Out here, with no water, we haven't got a hope."

"Go to sleep," she said. "It'll help clear your

mind. We don't know when we'll get the chance to rest again."

Amon dozed fitfully. How much longer could they continue sailing? They'd brought enough water for him and Lydia. Now they were sharing it with Hester and Marco as well, and Marco needed much more than his share. Amon licked his dry lips and felt the thick, sticky saliva in his mouth. He longed for a glass of water — to gulp it down and then have another.

He must have slept because, when he woke, it was with a start. The wind had dropped a little and, close by, he could hear a sound that was not unfamiliar. It was a small sound, a light scratching, and it was coming from the hull of the yacht behind his head.

The others were asleep. Amon pulled himself up on one elbow and looked behind him. It was the bird, at least it was *a* bird. Its feathers were pure white and it was marching back and forth along the hull, slipping and sliding on the polished resin surface. He reached out for it, but it flew up and into the sky.

It was not alone. A small flock of five or six of the creatures was circling above. They dipped and dived, playing on the wind, and came eventually to land a few metres away from where he was lying. They looked identical, pristine white, and each with bright beady eyes.

Amon stood up and walked toward the birds, crouching down when he was close to them. He held out his hand and waited. Eventually, one of the creatures strutted slowly towards him.

"Come on," he coaxed, "come to me."

The bird came close enough to peck at his fingernail. Then it hopped on to the back of his hand and, finally, walked up his arm to sit close to his face.

It felt enormously comforting to have it there against his skin, warm and silky. Very slowly, he reached across with his other hand and stroked the bird's feathers. It made a little cooing sound and seemed to settle more firmly on his shoulder. He ran his fingers down its legs, then up to where they met its body. The skin on one leg was rough. He parted the feathers and saw the scar.

"You're *my* bird," he breathed.

Suddenly, the birds on the ground flapped their wings and raised themselves into the air. Immediately, the bird on Amon's shoulder took

Chapter Twenty-two

flight and joined them as they circled above.

"Sorry," said Hester, coming over to him. "I think I disturbed them. They're so ...so beautiful."

"They are," Amon breathed. He looked at Hester. "The one that was sitting on my shoulder, I'm sure it's the one I looked after in Ledron."

"Do you think they might lead us back to wherever it is they've come from?" asked Hester.

Amon looked up at them, still circling. "It's possible," he said.

"Let's hurry then," she urged. "Let's get ready to go before they disappear."

But already, one of the birds was breaking away from the flock to return to the yachts.

"It's waiting for us," said Amon, as if not quite able to believe it. "I'm sure it is."

Lydia woke and stood up, shaking her head in disbelief when she saw the bird.

"It's been so long since I saw an animal," she breathed. "A bird! I can't believe it!"

"Amon thinks it's the same one that visited him back in Ledron," explained Hester.

"Marco?" Amon crouched over Marco, gently shaking him awake. "Marco? Marco!" He looked up with a frightened face. "I can't wake him!"

Hester rushed over. "Marco? Marco? Wake up!"

"His forehead," said Lydia, laying the back of her hand against his skin. "He's so hot. We have to cool him down."

"The water," said Hester. "Once he's in the yacht, I'll sponge his forehead. As we sail, the movement of the air will cool him."

"There's not much water left now," reminded Amon.

"What's left has to be for Marco," said Hester.

Together, they lifted him into the seat of the yacht. His head fell back limply. Amon rigged the sail as Lydia tore another strip from her shirt and soaked it in water. She passed it to Hester.

The bird, sensing they were about to leave, fluttered into the air and flew in circles above them.

"I hope you know where you're taking us," Amon whispered into the sky.

Chapter Twenty-three

Progress was slow. Every few minutes, Hester stopped to moisten Marco's forehead. Amon and Lydia said nothing to each other about their thirst, though their throats were so dry it was now difficult to swallow. With the last of their share of water, they moistened a cloth and applied it to their cracking lips.

"Any change in Marco?" asked Lydia as the yachts drew together.

Hester shook her head. "I don't know how much longer I can go on," she said. "I don't know how much longer *he* can travel for."

Amon had run out of reassuring words but, when they looked up, the bird was still above them, a solid reminder of their own hope. It was leading them in the direction Amon had expected to sail, but it was getting too dark to follow it.

"We'll keep going for as long as we can," he said.

It was when the light had finally faded that Lydia noticed something in the sky.

"There's some sort of glow up ahead — isn't there?" she asked. Her voice was a dry rasp. "It's faint, but there's something there — unless I'm imagining it."

Hester had seen it, too. She pointed into the distance as she sailed past them.

It seemed to Amon that the sky on the horizon had begun to shimmer. Or perhaps it was only a trick of the rising moon.

In that moment, the bird, which had been out of sight for some time, swooped down in front of the yacht and flew low ahead of them.

"Keep going!" Amon croaked to Hester. "Just keep going."

As they bounced across the uneven ground, the glow in the sky grew stronger until it was a halo of light in the distance. Amon was too tired and thirsty to be afraid of what they might encounter when they reached whatever was in front of them. His total concentration was fixed on reaching the source of light.

Chapter Twenty-three

"Keep it up," he encouraged Hester, sailing alongside her for a time. "Don't give up now."

The bird, coming and going from the front of the yachts, was like a song that drew them on.

"Wind generators!" said Lydia. "Look!"

Tall towers had appeared out of the darkness. The moon was now high in the sky and, in its silver light, they saw that, although they were much taller, the generators were not unlike those of Ledron.

In the distance, Amon could see the shape of enormous structures that glowed like fluorescent orbs. They were tall, higher than any buildings he had ever seen, and there were so many it was impossible to count them.

Something like excitement stirred in his chest. Perhaps they would be allowed to enter this place, be given water. But could they help Marco, or was it already too late?

When they were within half a kilometre of the city, which was how Lydia was now describing the settlement, the light in the sky was so intense that the bird could easily be seen flying above them.

Also distinguishable was the sail of a yacht tacking towards them. Their arrival had been observed.

Memories of the armed border patrol came flooding back, but Amon knew they had no choice but to go on. Behind them lay certain death. Hester dropped back and, as the craft approached, Amon brought his yacht to a halt.

"We're from Ledron," he managed to call as they came face to face with the sailor and his passenger.

"Ledron!" The woman in the passenger's seat seemed astonished. "Are there more of you?" she asked.

"Just us," said Amon. "We need water. Please, can you give us water?"

She nodded. "I'm Jessur," she said, reaching back into her yacht for a container. "You really are from Ledron?" she asked again.

Amon grabbed the container from her and passed it to Lydia. Hester drank next, then Amon.

"Our friend is injured," he said.

"It's his shoulder," said Hester. "He was injured when we crossed the border. He needs help – urgently."

"Follow us," said Jessur, quickly returning to

Chapter Twenty-three

her yacht. "There's nothing we can do here. We need to get him to a recovery centre." She leapt into her seat. "Stay close," she called back.

They followed the leader yacht and, on reaching the first of the glowing buildings, sailed into a walled courtyard. Wide glass doors in the lower storey of a squat dome slid back and a stretcher team rushed out to meet them.

"Gently now," said a woman who seemed to be in charge, as Marco was transferred to the stretcher.

"Where are you taking him? I want to go with him," said Hester.

"Sorry," said Jessur, "but we can't let you go anywhere at the moment."

As Marco was wheeled away, she showed them into a small room, unfurnished apart from a row of simple chairs.

"I have to go now," said Jessur, preparing to leave. "Don't be alarmed by the gas you'll hear entering the chamber." She pointed to a smoke-coloured vapour hissing from a floor vent. "It's non-toxic – just a decontamination requirement."

"But, Marco," pleaded Hester, frantically. "When can I see him?"

"I'm sorry," said Jessur, letting herself out the door. "Someone will be here soon to answer your questions."

Chapter Twenty-three

Chapter Twenty-four

"Welcome!"

Amon had been dozing in his chair and the deep voice startled him.

"Welcome to Oasis." And then, as if the stranger standing at the door was reading their thoughts: "Your friend is being cared for. There seems to be no doubt that he will recover."

"Can we see him?" asked Hester.

"Soon." The man smiled. "I am Titan. I'm here to make you comfortable and to answer your questions. Please, follow me."

He led them through a corridor that opened on to a vast glass dome where the air was warm and moist. The space was filled with low-growing ferns and bushes that sprouted bright flowers and fruit. But it was the trees that startled Amon. He had never seen any so tall. They stretched almost to the top of the glass ceiling sixty metres above.

"That's bird song," said Lydia, listening to the shrill chirpings and high-pitched musical calls all around them. "I remember it."

They crossed a low bridge that spanned a shallow stream.

"All that water!" puzzled Amon. "Where's it going? Who's guarding it?"

Hester let out a frightened squeal. "Something landed on my foot!"

Titan glanced back at the ground. "A small frog," he said. "Nothing to be afraid of."

Beneath a palm tree, dishes of fresh fruit and nuts and jugs of water had been set out for them.

"Sit," said Titan, gesturing to some chairs. "Drink all the water you want. We do not impose the restrictions that you are accustomed to."

Amon filled his glass.

"Control water and you can control an entire population," mused Titan as he watched them drink. "Tell me, how did you break through Ledron's border?"

"You know about the border patrol?" Hester asked.

Chapter Twenty-four

"We know a great deal about your community."

"Perhaps more than we know ourselves?"

He smiled at her. "I should think that is probably the case."

He listened intently as they told him of their escape.

"Of course," he said when they had finished, "it would interest us to know why it was that you decided to leave Ledron."

Amon shot a glance towards Lydia. It was too soon to mention her arm. They did not yet know if they would be allowed to stay.

"It was because of me," said Hester quickly. "I was making discoveries — discoveries that our Leaders would rather I hadn't made."

"And no doubt you risked 'retirement'," he said.

"You know about that?" she asked.

He nodded. "A barbaric practice." He studied their faces. "People here die a natural death. Unless they themselves choose otherwise. We care for the ill and frail. Our elderly live useful lives."

"You obviously have greater water supplies than we do," suggested Lydia.

He shook his head. "Our water is as limited as your own. But we have allowed our greatest minds to work towards its conservation." He gestured towards the trees. "This is the result. Oasis is a series of biodomes — closed systems that continually filter and recirculate moisture."

"Ledron could have the same," said Hester bitterly, "if the Leaders encouraged it."

"Your Leaders depend upon the rationing of water to maintain their power and control," said Titan. "They will do anything to prevent discoveries or inventions that make water more readily available."

He helped himself to a ripe plum.

"After the water wars," he said, "it is true that complete control in the hands of a few was the only way to ensure immediate order and survival. However, as the situation improved, most communities chose a more democratic path towards progress."

"But not Ledron," guessed Amon.

"Ledron's Leaders had tasted a power they were not willing to give up. As the communities around them grew more open, Ledron cut off communication."

"You mean, *power* is what keeps them doing what they do?"

"Power, ultimate control. It's like a drug to them — addictive, impossible to give up."

"The border patrol," said Hester. "It's there to keep others out, not to keep us in, isn't it? That's why, once we were heading away from Ledron, the guard yachts didn't keep chasing us."

"Why would your people wish to escape?" asked Titan. "They do not believe there is anywhere to escape *to*. However, those who are free feel an obligation to liberate those who are not."

"They were training Marco to fight on the border," she said. "No wonder he wouldn't have lived long."

"There are many communities in existence – we know of forty – and, yes, although our own means of making contact are purely peaceful, others do use force in an attempt to reach your people. If your intention had been to break through the border *into* Ledron, you would have found yourselves surrounded by guard yachts."

"The bird I discovered in Ledron," said Amon slowly. "It was your way of making peaceful contact, wasn't it?"

Titan nodded. "We have a scientist here, a highly innovative thinker. He has spent years breeding homing pigeons to be particularly inquisitive – to fly further than usual and to rely on very little water. He calls them the 'camels of the air'. Very recently, we began to suspect that they were flying as far as Ledron. It is our hope that they will continue to breach the border and that the messages they carry to your people will eventually destabilise Ledron's Leadership."

"It could work," said Amon. "Slowly but surely, it might work."

Lydia moved uncomfortably in her chair. "You seem to know a great deal about our community and how it operates," she said. "Perhaps we are not the first to have escaped from Ledron."

"Ah," said Titan. "I wondered when you might ask about this." He paused, as if considering how best to explain. "The scientist responsible for the bird programme," he began, "was a political refugee – the only person from Ledron that we know of, apart from yourselves, to have escaped."

"When did he arrive?" asked Amon.

"Thirteen years ago. We found him close to death, travelling in a sand yacht that he had built himself. Unlike you, he had no knowledge of the existence of other communities. He had simply fled, on the spur of the moment, to escape 'retirement.'"

Something stirred in the back of Amon's mind – the strangest idea. But it was impossible . . .

"The bird man," he said slowly. "Would it be possible to meet him? To thank him?"

"Of course," said Titan. "I'll bring him to you immediately."

He raised himself up from his seat and took a path that led back the way they had come.

"We've been living a lie," said Hester, shaking her head. "Our entire community has been living an artificial existence. A horrible, huge lie."

"Why didn't we ever question anything? That's what I can't understand," said Amon.

"Some tried," insisted Hester. "And we know what happened to them."

"Ahem." Titan cleared his throat to announce his return. A tall, bearded man with glasses stood, rather shyly, beside him.

"Allow me to introduce you to our 'bird man'," he said. "Doctor King."

Amon's eyes flicked towards Lydia. She showed no signs of recognition, but the man was studying her intently.

"Lydia?" he ventured at last.

At the sound of his voice, she started.

"You *are* Lydia — aren't you?"

She made no reply. Hester looked at Amon.

"You don't recognise me, do you?" said the man.

"*Malory* King?" asked Amon. "Are you . . .?"

"Malory?" said Lydia faintly.

Her face was white and she held tightly to the arm of her chair.

"Yes, yes, it's me." He crossed the room. His hand was shaking as he reached out to take hers.

"You *know* each other?" asked Titan.

"What's going on?" Hester hissed at Amon.

"Malory King." Amon said the words softly to himself, as if testing them out for the first time.

"You . . . you look so different," whispered Lydia.

"You haven't changed," said Malory.

"Amon," she said, but Amon interrupted her.

"It's all right. I know what you're going to say." He stood up and took a step towards them both. "I'm Amon," he said, introducing himself to the man. "And I know who you are. You're my father."

It was so unreal to be embraced by someone who was your father and, at the same time, a stranger, but Amon let himself sink into the arms that were thrown about him.

"Ledron took you away from me," said Malory. "But the birds have brought you back. I knew they would, but I never dreamt it would be this soon. I never dared to hope that you might be the first."

When Amon joined Hester at Marco's bedside later in the evening, Marco was sitting up, talking to her, a narrow tube dripping liquid into a vein in one arm.

"Awesome news," said Marco. "I can't get my head around it."

"Neither can I," said Amon. "Mum didn't even recognise my father at first, not with his beard and glasses. She says he looks much older."

"Why did he leave Ledron?" asked Hester.

"The yacht he was working on, it would have enabled travel for hundreds — maybe thousands of kilometres," explained Amon. "It would have enabled Ledron to explore for water. But, in exploring for water, other communities might have been discovered. A yacht like the one my father was working on was a threat to Ledron's isolation."

"But he left without telling you," said Hester.

"He didn't have time to tell my mother he was going. One night, on the way to the yacht house, a friend gave him a tip-off that he was to be retired. The Secure Division was already out looking for him. So he just left, on the only yacht he had. He had no food, no water, nothing. He didn't even know that there were other communities out here."

"And, after he'd gone, they made up that story about his having been ill?" asked Marco.

Amon nodded. Then he smiled. "When my father got to the border, he just bluffed his way through the patrol. Every top sailor knew him, admired him. He was famous for his work on the racers. So my dad, he just told the patrol guards that he was trialling a new model and that he had permission to take the yacht further out into the desert for an endurance test. He told them he'd be back in an hour."

"That is so smart!" said Marco with a laugh. "Hester said the birds are his idea, too. A peaceful

Chapter Twenty-four

way of infiltrating Ledron and destabilising the Leaders."

Amon nodded. "When enough people in Ledron receive messages and begin asking questions, there'll eventually be action."

"Your father must be an amazing man," said Marco.

Amon nodded. "I only wish I could have known him all those years ago."

The door to Marco's room opened and Lydia came in. "We really need to get some rest now, all of us," she said. "We've been allocated rooms. And," she smiled, "we've been offered a shower."

"A what?" asked Amon.

"A shower," repeated Lydia. "I've just had one. It's a most delightful experience."

"What's a shower?" asked Hester suspiciously.

"Come with me," said Lydia. "I'll show you."

Amon smiled. It was so long since he had seen Lydia happy. Her laughter sounded like music.

EPILOGUE

Lydia

With medical help, Lydia survived a further eight years. She worked in the public gardens of Oasis, tending the flowers she had always dreamed of growing.

Marco

Marco recovered to sail again. As a steady trickle of refugees began fleeing from Ledron, he was employed to go into the desert to guide them to the safety of welcoming communities. He returned, eventually, to live with Hester in Ledron after the overthrow of the Leaders.

Hester

Hester continued her research into closed systems, developing further the mechanisms that are in use at Oasis. When the Leadership at Ledron was eventually destabilised and the Leaders overthrown, she was one of the first professors at the community's new School of Bioscience.

Amon
Amon worked with his father to breed and train the birds that would eventually free the people of Ledron. When the project was no longer needed, he returned to Ledron to establish colonies of birds in its new biodomes.